Abandoned but not Forsaken

A true story.

D1565665

BY
DANA CRYER

Abandoned but not Forsaken
ISBN: 978-1-936314-80-5
© 2012 by Dana Cryer

Published by Word and Spirit Publishing
P.O. Box 701403
Tulsa, Oklahoma 74170

CONTENTS

Preface
My Prayer for You

I am so excited for the opportunity to share my story with so many wonderful people. I believe through the Holy Spirit and God's healing grace, lives will be changed. "Therefore if any man be in Christ, he is a new creature: old things are passed away, behold, all things are become new" (2 Corinthians 5:17). What this means is that those who become Christians are changed. They are not the same anymore, for the old life is gone. A new life has begun!

My prayer for you is that you will trust God and his Holy Spirit to speak to you today. And I speak peace to your heart, that your heart will open and receive love—the love only God can give us. Yes, we are blessed with family, mates, and friends. But God's love is the beginning of how to give and receive love. God is love.

I pray that I will be able to bless people by telling my story and that those who hear or read my story will be over-comers in their own lives. Everyone has something to give others. God loves each and everyone the same because he is not a respecter of persons.

PART ONE

My Story

I will not in any way fail your nor give you up nor leave you without support. I will not, I will not, I will not in any degree leave you helpless nor forsake nor let you down, relax My hold on you! Assuredly not!

—Hebrews 13;5b AMP

November 5, 1946

In the middle of the day in a hospital in Flagstaff, Arizona, I was born in the usual way as any other baby would be. The only unusual thing about my birth was that after bringing me into this world, my mother left me . . . at the hospital! The one thing I possessed was an incomplete birth certificate, handwritten "unnamed baby girl" with the name of my father left blank; the name of my mother erroneous.

I was abandoned as an infant. No identity. No bonding with my mother. No comforting cuddles. No adoring grandparents or devoted aunts or uncles, and no fond memories of a normal childhood. In fact, I have no memories at all of the time between my birth and the day a man named Pete came into my life when I was five years old.

Life As a Victim

My very first memory begins one particular day when I was just five years old. A man named Pete approached me while I was on the playground. He must have told me something very inviting, because I willingly got into his old beat-up station wagon with a small, shiny silver trailer hooked to it. As it turned out, later I would be left alone in that tiny trailer countless times to fend for myself. But I remember right off, this man from the playground started having sex with me. This man was my father.

Life with Pete

Pete lived in an old white house up in the mountains and had sex with me all the time. Morning, noon, and night. One day followed the next, each one just like the one before it. He was rough and heavy, forcing me to do things I did not want to do. I had no choice. Never, ever, was I around anyone else. For the next few years, Pete kept me isolated.

During those years of seclusion, I did not attend school. I had no ability to read or write. I did not know that 1+1=2. I did not know red and yellow make orange. There were no bedtime stories or favorite children's books. There were no playmates, no toys, no dolls. No holidays or birthdays were celebrated. I did not run and play in the sunshine, nor watch TV or listen to music. Pete kept me to himself.

Because I was so young when it all started, my entire being was shaped by my father. I didn't know anything differently. My existence was just sex all the time and focusing solely on taking care of Pete's needs. I had no life, no options, no security, and certainly no love. What I had was plenty of confusion and fear. And fear is darkness. I clearly remember the blank darkness surrounding me while it was pounded into my head over and over: "Do not tell!"

For about four years, Pete kept me completely captive to do what he desired when he desired. My young mind could not comprehend, could not answer whether this was right or wrong. But because Pete kept threatening to kill me if I told anyone, this must be wrong. And because he kept telling me that I was a pig, that I was ugly and fat (even though I wasn't), and that I would never amount to anything, I began to think there must be something wrong with me.

Stealing to Live

Pete's existence was one defined by sex and constant drinking. He always smelled of liquor; he continually was drunk. Besides that, not only did he use foul language all the time, he was also a compulsive liar. He lied about everything, which in turn taught me to do the same.

So it was when I was about 7 years old and when I should have been in school like other children my age, that Pete began driving around during the day looking for things to steal: bicycles, tricycles, and things of value like that, mostly from oil well sites and farmhouses. He would scout out other people's property in the daylight, then go back at night to load up his station wagon with all the items that would fit.

This was how Pete supported himself and his drinking habit. (Of course there was never a thought of me having a bicycle or anything like that. I would not have known how to ride one anyway!) As a result, Pete lived a life of continual running. He was always peeling out of parking lots and speeding down roads for fear of being caught.

Eventually, Pete began to use me to help him steal. He knew just the times to go plundering when no one would be around. Sometimes, because I was smaller and quicker, I would have to climb fences and open gates. Sometimes there would be dogs barking. Then, after carrying off all the plunder we could find, the next day Pete would promptly sell the stolen things to pawn shops, take the money, and head off to the bars.

Lots of times when I was with him during these trips to spy out the goods, it would turn into night and I would have to sleep in the car while Pete was drinking in a bar. It did not matter to him whether the weather was hot or cold. It did not matter to him whether I was hungry or afraid, nor that I was left alone in the back seat of his car. He just made sure to tell me adamantly that I could not utter one word to anyone of what he was doing to me or that he was stealing stuff. Again, during all this time I was never around other people. Pete kept me isolated.

However, there was one incident among many in which my father, following his customary night of drinking, was picked up, arrested, and put into jail for D.U.I. Since I was also in his car, the police put me in a jail cell, too. The next cell over from his! Were the police really protecting me? Did they care about my welfare? Could they not see how I was being treated? But then, I would not have told them the truth. I was too afraid to tell. I had to remain a captive in my confusing, painful life.

Mary's House

Then one day an unexpected trip took place. Pete took me to a house where there were other children and a lady named Mary. Pete told me again that I could never say anything, which I never did out of fear—the fear that had become my constant, unwanted companion. You see, among his other dreadful behaviors, Pete had a horrible temper. And he had a gun. He would kill me if I said anything. Needless to say, I was very afraid of him and learned not to show any disobedience or emotion toward him.

At Mary's house, I was the oldest among the other children. There was Helen, who was nine months younger than I, and Earl, Robert, and James. Pete and Mary would leave us there alone on occasion. I remember many times standing on a chair with Helen to reach the stove in the kitchen, sometimes cooking gravy for dinner or whatever I could find. So not only did I have to meet all of Pete's demands, I, as a nine-year-old child, would be left in charge of also caring for these other children.

It became a regular, frightening occurrence that whenever Pete and Mary were together they would fight. Furniture would sometimes get thrown around and broken. At these times, I would take the children and try to hide them from all the screaming and fighting. Pete would be violent with Mary, but fortunately not toward me or the other four children. Things would get so bad between them that I remember hiding with the other children in a dog house in the back yard, until—routinely it seemed—the police would come and take Pete to jail.

Then Pete and I would leave for awhile, but we would always go back to Mary's house. It turns out, Pete was married to Mary and had fathered these other children. Mary was not my biological mother, but my stepmother. And although she was to be my mother figure, Mary never offered me loving care or nurturing assurance. There were no hugs or touches of affection. Not once did I hear "I love you, Dana. Come sit on my lap." I saw nothing of a normal family life.

However, when we would stay at Mary's place for awhile, Pete always made sure I slept closest to the door where he would have me slip out and go somewhere in the house secretly for sex. Other times I would have to sleep with the window open and he would tap on the window to signal for me to crawl out. Not surprisingly, I was always afraid to go to sleep and would constantly be thinking, *will he come for me tonight?*

A Texas Cellar

When I was ten years old, Pete, Mary, my four half-siblings, and myself all moved to a house in Texas. I do not remember whether there were neighbors or how isolated the house may have been. Regardless, Pete began taking me to the cellar of the house. I do remember how big, abrupt, and heavy he felt while having sex with me and the tremendous fear, dread, and confusion I felt from not being able to control what was being done to me.

But one day, a day I remember was sunny and beautiful, I was outside playing with the other children. Clothes were flapping on the clothesline in the gentle breeze. Tumbleweeds were blowing by. Pete, however, interrupted that fine day by showing up and taking me again to the cellar. Horror filled my being. Would this never end?

But it was on this particular day that Mary decided to go to the cellar herself. She casually opened the cellar door only to discover what Pete was doing to me. Immediately, she ran back into the house and got a gun. As Pete fled from the cellar, she shot him. The bullet grazed his leg, leaving a bloody trail as he ran off into the canyon behind the house.

In no time, the police were there to apprehend Pete, then promptly took me to the hospital. It was cold and lonely in that examination room. More fright and confusion followed, as I still remember the doctor who examined me pronouncing that I would probably never have children of my own and that I would definitely have serious mental problems.

Pete's Arrest

With Pete in police custody, I was taken to a temporary place until the State decided what to do. I was yanked from the only familiarity I had and placed into an interim home—a place of real isolation; a holding place for abused kids just like me. I remember lots of bunk beds in one large room filled with crying kids. I was held there for close to six months. No TV was permitted for me due to the massive media coverage taking place at that time with regard to my situation. The shame hidden so long was now coming to light.

While at this home I had to be taught the basics of life, like hygiene and bathing. I'm sure I looked a sight to behold and must have sounded like one, too! In fact, I discovered later that court records reported me as "poor white trash." Another strike against my identity. But I did not know life any other way.

The day finally came when I had to go to court and be a witness against my father. The State found him guilty and sent him to prison. During the trial, I was terrified to make eye contact with him, but when I did, he angrily mouthed, "I'll get you!" Pete was still exerting control and causing the frightening dread I had known so very well from living with him those long, past five years.

Days later the court decided what to do with me and Mary's four children. While we were assembled out front of the courthouse, a boy's ranch van picked up Earl and Robert. A sheriff car came next for James, who was about 5 years old and too young to be placed with his brothers in the boys' home. I remember that frightened little boy to this day. He was screaming and kicking as they were carrying him off to put in the car. A teddy bear had been placed in the back seat of the car. But James, loudly crying out for me, was not to be consoled by any stuffed animal.

Another car then arrived to pick up Helen and myself to take us to a children's home in Amarillo, Texas. It was then, at age eleven, I entered the school system by being placed directly in the fifth grade. Remember, I had never been to school before! It was another horribly difficult time in my life.

On top of all this drama, at the same time Helen and I were placed in that children's home, my stepmother, Mary, got really sick. We were taken to the hospital to see her. We entered her hospital room to find that she was barely alive and encased inside an oxygen tent. She looked so bad. She could only write us notes to communicate, because at this point she could no longer talk. She was covered with cancer and dying. Oh, the pain we felt. Everything had been taken from us. First our three brothers and now Mary. We watched our brothers being taken away by strangers, then we watched Mary being taken away by sickness, for she died while we were in her presence. Her obituary simply stated that she died from a two-week illness.

An Angelic Visitation

That night after our painful visit at the hospital, Helen and I were taken back to the children's home. The home was such that there were three girls to a room and Helen and I were placed together as roommates. That night after the hospital visit and after the lights had been turned off, I was in my bed crying. So much pent-up emotion had to be released. Everything was confusing. My world was shaken. The darkness was not a welcome companion and I felt oh so alone, abandoned once again.

But then the room got bright! I could only think that my house mother had turned on the light. Yet it wasn't that kind of light. The next thing I saw was an angel standing at the foot of my bed. The brightness was something I will never forget! Streams of light were as tall as the ceiling and the angel was very white. He was beautiful. The angel then said to me, "Jesus loves you and will always be with you." Thinking Helen saw and heard all of this, I couldn't wait to talk about it with her the next morning, but she didn't see or hear anything.

Even though I didn't know Jesus and had not heard of him, I knew something significant had happened. An angel visited me! I tucked this special visitation into my heart and would much later have that same message repeated to me at a critical turning point in my life.

Life at School

I struggled so hard with school—going from absolutely no schooling of any kind to being placed straight into the fifth grade was torture! Remember, I did not even know simple math or the names of things or even the ABC'S. How horrible that all the kids could see how dumb I was.

The teacher would always call on me in the classroom but I never, ever had the answer. I always felt a total blackness in my head. This occurred because I had learned years earlier to show no emotion. I could not even show tears. So my way of coping was to hold everything inside. The most reaction I would show would be clenching my fists. When Pete was having sex with me, I began doing that. Then at other challenging times, I would clench my fists often to the point of blacking out in my mind.

What was building on the inside eventually would come to the outside and I would black out. My mind would shut down and enter into blackness. I would be overcome with fear and panic so strong that I literally would not be able to hear or see for awhile. That would happen anytime I felt unsure or fearful, whether at the children's home or at school or practically anywhere.

It was also pointed out to me that when I walked, I clutched my shirt near the neckline with my fists clenched and that even while I was sitting, my fists would be clenched in front of me. It got to the point that the superintendent over the school talked to me about how scared I was at school and about being around other girls and boys my age. But to me, it was awful knowing that these kids could plainly see the problems I had and how far behind I was. Even the teachers seemed not to have patience with me.

Therefore, during my school years I don't remember ever having any friends. I just remember facing more rejection, more feelings of loneliness, and not fitting in. No one liked me; no one wanted me. *Something is wrong with me,* I thought, having believed that from early on in my life. So much so, in fact, that one day in my future this belief would lead me to make a drastic, nearly lethal decision.

Incessant Violation

To add further pain and fear, certain men would attempt to make sexual advances toward me whenever I was left alone in their care, whether at the children's home or on the way to the dentist or to visit an attorney or wherever! Men continued to exert such control over me. I grew so scared. Great fear—that unwanted companion—came into my life again. Along with that, was an overwhelming feeling of dread and horror at having no control over what was being done to me. Would I never be free from this?

The very worst aspect of this continuing behavior toward me was that my very own father—after serving his prison sentence—would be permitted to visit me at the home and try to molest me right there. Unbelievable! He hadn't changed and he had an uncanny way of locating me.

You see, once a month after church, visitation from friends and family would take place at the children's home where Helen and I lived. Every Sunday, all the kids would get on a bus to attend the local Presbyterian church that sponsored the home. The boys had to dress nicely and the girls were required to wear dresses, so I would be attired that way.

Certain rooms within the home were designated for those times of visitation and in which the child would have privacy with their visitor. Because of this standard procedure, I would be left alone wearing a little dress, behind a closed door in one of these visitation rooms with Pete—my father; a man with a record of previous crimes against me! In this private room, every now and then someone from the home would check in, but that did not stop my father from trying to touch me inappropriately, nor stop the kissing he forced upon me. Oh, the torment! Pete was still exerting his awful ways over me. Was there anyone anywhere to protect me?

Life at the Home

There were times during my stay at the home when we would be taken to a basement where people from the community donated clothes for the children living there. This created further cause for embarrassment for me going to school. I was nothing like the other kids. I had no parents. No house to call home. No friends. No regular clothes. And no previous schooling! Plus, I had the painful rejection from potential parents who came to view us for adoption. I can only say my school years were bad for me.

But I had one special teacher who cared. I trusted him enough to talk about some of the things that had happened to me. God bless him. He would stay after school trying to help me learn something, even while Mother Mae from the home was telling me that learning the basics of math and reading would be a skill I would probably never be able to master. In fact, she would take out a ping pong paddle covered with duct tape and paddle me every time she saw my report card!

That one caring teacher however, knew my lack of previous schooling was why I would almost black out and not know what to say or how to answer questions in the classroom. He could see the fear that would take over. But fear also came from a lifetime of abuse and abandonment. Maybe he even knew that, as well.

I have thought so many times as an adult that as a child, my mind just could not comprehend what was happening to me. Pete's years of abuse toward me and that of various other men as well caused me to feel dirty, scared, and fearful of what people thought of me or might do to me. On top of that, all through my limited years of schooling, I could scarcely read or write. I would later be asked by different people, "How did you graduate?" "Nobody knows!" I would reply. Nevertheless, I was blessed to have graduated from high school in 1965 and to get married to a loving man shortly after that.

A Trustworthy Man

While still in high school, Helen and I attended a local dance. It was there that I met my future husband, Gene. He became my first real boyfriend and the love of my life. The moment I saw him, I liked him and thought he was cute. It was truly "love at first sight" for he cared about me and loved me immensely (and still does to this day!). He wanted me to be his wife.

So the time came when I had to leave the children's home after graduation from school at age seventeen. A foster family took me in because I simply had nowhere to go and no money to get there. I had no plans for my future. I had no self-esteem. But Gene's family, after he told them about me, took me in as one of their own children and loved me, no questions asked. This was the first time for me to experience love of family. Even though Gene's mother already had six children, she loved all of them and me just the same. She was the most sweet, loving, nurturing woman there ever was and never complained or had a mean word about anyone. I wanted to be just like her when I grew up.

Because we were engaged to be married, it became necessary for me to tell Gene about my incestuous past. It was only right to tell him and his parents my story. TV news and local newspapers were filled with the events of my past life anyway. Who in that small town didn't already know of the little girl with the abusive father?

I greatly loved and trusted Gene and felt safe in his presence. If anything, his knowledge of my abusive father caused him to become even closer to me. So on May 15, 1965, Gene and I were married. Here I was, eighteen years old and I had never heard the words "I love you." I had never heard words of affirmation from anyone. Because of this, I did not even know how to say "I love you, Gene." Oh, the things I had to learn!

Uninvited Fear

During the early days of our marriage, Gene did shift work for the oil industry. This meant often being home by myself at night, which was dreadful for me. Despite the deep love Gene and I had for one another and how deeply we thought of each other, torment had not departed my mind. Knowing full well my father was released from prison and very likely to have located me, I was always looking over my shoulder. My mind continually relived scenes from my past life with him and I was always wondering if my father was nearby. Too terrified to sleep with my back to the door in my own apartment or close to any window, I was also unable to sleep when Gene wasn't home.

What especially kept my father's memory and impending presence alive was that Gene and I would find out from others in that small Texas town that Pete was fathering more children. Another baby would be birthed with his last name! And many other things would trigger uncomfortable memories of my past life. Just seeing a small silver

Airstream camper being towed would cause my mind to go right back to those frightening days of being left alone in one at the age of five.

In fact, my father did intrude into my life at this time. Through his uncanny way of locating me, he let me know he had found me by first making phone calls. I could only slam down the phone not wanting any contact with him. Then he knocked on my door one day, but I wanted nothing to do with him. He even somehow got our credit card number and had the audacity to spend a huge amount of money. We had no recourse but to file a protective order against him.

Needless to say, Gene hated my father. But he thought to get a dog for me and so one day brought home a German Shepherd we named Derrick, who was from then on always with me. The dog's presence was comforting and gave me the sense of security I needed to be able to sleep.

Against All Odds

I had always wanted to be a mother, but along with that normal, natural desire, I was severely tormented with thoughts of never being able to bear children. Well, God had another plan. In spite of what had been done to my young body and what doctors may have said, our first son, Brent, was born April 30, 1968!

Not knowing at the time his future was already planned, someone put a little toy golf set in his baby bed at the hospital when he was born. Someone else brought him a set of yellow Ben Hogan baby clothes that he wore home from the hospital. You see, Brent later went on to become a golf pro!

Then our second son, Brad, was born June 16, 1972. What a sweet baby, very quiet. Brad just naturally chose to play with toy airplanes when he was quite young. As he grew older, he took flying lessons and became a flight attendant!

Both boys have always respected and loved me. I can truly say, I never one time had a desire to harm my little boys in any way sexually. I know that can be a generational curse but thank God, I *never* thought about harming them. Without a doubt, my babies were a gift from God.

The Persevering Neighbor

We moved to Pampa, Texas, when the boys were young. A couple living across the street from our house invited me and my family to church, but only Brent and Brad would go. The boys loved it and became born again there. When they would come home, they would tell me the church was praying that I would get born again, but I wanted nothing to do with all that. My heart had a hard shell around it. I just wasn't in the least interested in any church. I was only interested in pursuing my own way of life, which included drinking and parties with people who liked to drink.

That hard shell was not softened even after an incident when my boys were five and nine years old, when almost any mother would have been touched in her heart. It was one particular day when I heard a sound like crying coming from the garage. I rushed in there only to find that my boys were inside a large cardboard box tearfully praying that their mother would get born again. But what did I do? I angrily told them to stop, to come out of there and never do that again.

Plus, in spite of all the kindness shown to me, my heart had no interest in Marilyn either, the neighbor who graciously took my boys to church every Sunday. But I carefully watched her life for two or three years. As I think back, she was the first Christian influence I had known, yet my stance was to avoid her! I would make every attempt to hide when I saw her coming. I would avoid answering the door when she knocked. Why was she always so peaceful and kind? Why was she always playing that gospel music in her car? Why did she have to keep cheerfully inviting me to church with her? Why was she so happy all the time? I only felt conviction around her with my dirty mouth and way of life, yet all the while she was loving me and praying for me.

In fact, Marilyn and her husband never preached at me and never judged me. Amidst all the drinking parties at my house, which they would sometimes attend but not drink alcohol, they walked in the true, unconditional love of God toward me. Marilyn's life shone brightly with the love of God. Yet all the while, I could only think how strange she was, talking about all this Jesus stuff, even though it was she who had so much peace and such a good life.

Marilyn, on the other hand, never lost hope. She was always asking me to go somewhere—places where people just like her would be—to which I would always say no. But for some reason, one time when asked to go to a tent meeting, I finally agreed and accompanied her. I had never been to anything like that—a Pentecostal church meeting out in the country in a tent! There were tambourines and dancing, tongue-talking and fiery preaching. My eyes must have stayed wide open the entire evening. But this was just a foretaste of what was to take place in my life a few days later.

Life at the Factory

Prior to these divine encounters with Marilyn and shortly after moving to Pampa, I took a job at a factory. Yet deep down inside I was so very unhappy in life. I secretly wanted my life to be over. At the factory, I was always crying from feeling so stupid and at times from not understanding what was happening around me. Plus, I felt like an empty shell of a person, oppressed, dirty, and downtrodden. All the while though, my boys were in church telling people that their mom needed to be born again. People were there at that church who cared about me and prayed for me without ever meeting me. Those prayers were soon to be actualized.

Enemy Temptation

Work at the factory was just as you might imagine. Everyday I stood in an assembly line, my coworkers and I just an arm's length apart. However, we could not talk to each other; we could only focus on the methodical routine of accurately filling our quota. But even if we could talk to one another, it was *so* loud in there as to be impossible to hear what was being said. As loud as the machinery was and as repetitive as the manual labor was, a sound more loud and repetitive was the one in my own head.

Remember, I felt unlearned, unclean, and unimportant. A pattern of wrong thinking had grown in me since childhood and it only grew worse during this time. Anger and hatred coupled with fear and self-doubt, along with self-loathing and unforgiveness were a recipe for self-destruction waiting to happen.

So it was inevitable that a continual barrage of tormenting thoughts plagued my mind day after day with voices that told me to kill myself. Voices that grew louder and louder telling me, "Just walk in front of a truck. Why not go jump in the nearby lake?" The voices were so strong that I could actually feel a presence on my shoulder talking in my ear all the time saying "just kill yourself."

One particular day while at the factory, the torment was so overpowering that I just had to leave my place at the assembly line and go into the restroom. I looked into a mirror to see a distorted, wild look on my face and in my eyes. I looked terrorized. Instantly I started screaming, "Stop! What is this? What is happening to me?" What was happening was lying spirits were tormenting me with their fear.

After so many episodes like this, the time came that I believed those relentless thoughts. Suicide began to seem like the only solution. Terminating my life would be the only way to put an end to my shame and confusion once and for all. Fear and torment would end also.

So one evening at home when Gene took the boys to football practice, I decided to pursue the plans to end my life. As I did, it was as if every detail to carry out this deed was given me in a script to follow, such as in a movie, even to the point of putting a red spread on the bed. Plus, I had made it a point to clean the house really well that weekend because I knew people would eventually be coming in there to find me dead. I even thought the red spread on the bed where I would die wouldn't be so hard to clean since it was as red as my spilled blood would be. Now, I just needed to get a gun and I knew where one was. I would end my life with a gunshot. Just a few footsteps away was a gun. . . .

God's Intervention

However, just as I was starting down the hall to get the gun, my mind intent on killing myself, the phone rang. It was Marilyn, of all people. Marilyn, the neighbor from across the street who had been taking my sons to church and from whom I used to hide, called to tell me that Jesus loved me and would never leave me. That was all she said, making this the second time I had heard this message from God. Upon hearing this from Marilyn, I instantly thought of the angelic visitation I had had while in the children's home, as the exact words were spoken to me then.

We hung up the phone and as I went back into my bedroom, the room suddenly lit up with the same kind of light from an angel like I had seen as a child! I tell you, I had some serious problems. But when I went into my bedroom, I had such a visitation. Bright light streamed down to fill my room and I heard a heavenly choir. It felt like a hand gently pushed me down onto my bed. So there on the red bedspread laid out for an entirely different purpose, I cried a hard, deep weeping for a long time.

God was there and I wanted him. Oh, how I now wanted him! I was truly at the end of myself and could now receive God. All his glory, all that God is, was in that room. That room was saturated with so much of God's love, I easily asked him to come into my heart. And thanks to all the times my sons would rush home from church excitedly telling me about God's free gift of salvation, I knew what to do. "If you confess with your mouth that Jesus is Lord and believe in your heart that God raised him from the dead, you will be saved. For it is by believing in your heart that you are made right with God, and it is by confessing with your mouth that you are saved" (Romans 10:9-10 NLT).

The New Birth

There was never a time in my life that I cried like that, so deeply and for so long that it turned into groaning. I was feeling such deep-seated pain—pain which spanned a lifetime. I had never experienced anything like this depth of release. Then the love I felt pouring into my heart was so wonderful! I had so much anger, so much hatred and negative emotion inside that I was not able to cry to that degree. My heart had turned to stone and could not release anything buried so deeply. Remember, my father had prevented me from ever showing emotion. Believe me, October 2, 1978, I wept. Hurtful things were being pulled out of me, while God's love poured into me.

While this was happening in my heart, Marilyn was prompted to come to my house. When she arrived, she explained that shortly after phoning me, God had told her to come to my house and pray with me. She got to share in the awesome experience of a life in transformation.

But before she arrived, the godly presence in my bedroom felt like someone was getting ready to touch me. And at that moment, even though I did not know one thing about Jesus or the Holy Spirit, my hands went up and while crying, some sounds came out of my mouth I could not identify! "And they were all filled with the Holy Ghost, and began to speak with other tongues, as the Spirit gave them utterance" (Acts 2:4 KJV).

I had been born again. "For God loved the world so much that he gave his one and only Son, so that everyone who believes in him will not perish but have eternal life" (John 3:16 NLT). I had become spiritually changed. "This means that anyone who belongs to Christ has become a new person. The old life is gone; a new life has begun!" (2 Corinthians 5:17 NLT). The saving power and awesome love and mercy of God through Jesus Christ transformed such a hideous life into a life like his. His salvation provided such cleansing from feeling dirty; such overflowing peace from tormenting fear; such abundance of joy from humiliating shame; such soundness of mind from relentless unrest; and such limitless love from bitter hatred. My stony heart had become softened.

When Marilyn arrived at my house, she began to cry with joy over me. We prayed together; we celebrated together the greatest miracle anyone can experience in life: the free gift of salvation. "But God is so rich in mercy, and he loved us so much, that even though we were dead because of our sins, he gave us life when he raised Christ from the dead. (It is only by God's grace that you have been saved!)" (Ephesians 2:4-5 NLT). And Scripture also says, "God saved you by his grace when you believed. And you can't take credit for this; it is a gift from God. Salvation is not a reward for the good things we have done, so none of us can boast about it" (Ephesians 2:8-9 NLT).

The next morning, I had to find the Bible Gene bought for me years earlier. I was now seeking life, not death! And with all this, a new interest and love for the Word of God was compelling me. "Thy words were found, and I did eat them; and thy word was unto me the joy and rejoicing of mine heart" (Jeremiah 15:16a KJV). Neither could I wait to get into church.

As soon as the next service time began, Marilyn took me to church with her family and my boys. I walked into the church only to find everyone was celebrating—celebrating what had just happened to me! Not only that, they had water baptism ready for me! It was there that I met a wonderful, loving pastor and his wife, Susie, who upon meeting me took me in with open arms and acceptance. Susie befriended me right away and began to call me often to pray with me and to ask if I had questions.

After a lifetime of despair and mental suffering, fear and shame, within one week's time I experienced the awesomeness of God first at a tent meeting, then in my bedroom, and now at a loving church. It was only the beginning of an inspiring, fulfilling, and purposeful life with God. He had many things yet to show me and do with me.

Dreams from God

This new life with God through Jesus, his Son, continued with God giving me dreams. The very first dream was simply amazing and revealed to me how real God is in each and every person's life no matter the circumstances, no matter the depravity or the prosperity. I dreamed that I was walking toward a big white house. On the front porch, I saw a man rocking a baby, rubbing the baby's back. I could hear him telling the baby how much he loved the baby. As I walked closer I knew it was Jesus. The baby then turned and looked at me. The baby was me! Wow. God moved so fast to help me know who he was in my new life. I could not wait to call Susie, my pastor's wife.

Maybe two nights later I had another dream, I was at home and lots of people were coming into my house. I noticed everyone was rolling up their pant legs before they entered. When they came in, water rose up to their knees. There was much joy and laughter among the people in my house. "Jesus replied, 'If you only knew the gift God has for you and who you are speaking to, you would ask me, and I would give you living water'" (John 4:10 NLT).

I called Susie again and told her about the dream. She said it was the Holy Spirit with springs of living water— a cleansing, a healing. "But those who drink the water I give will never be thirsty again. It becomes a fresh, bubbling spring within them, giving them eternal life" (John 4:14 NLT).

Exciting things were happening to me. To me! Just a week of new life in Christ. I knew it was a good thing, a true thing. "The teaching of your word gives light, so even the simple can understand" (Psalm 119:130 NLT). And God was always waking me during the night to tell me something. One of the first things he spoke to me was, "Eyes and ears; eyes and ears." I thought, *What? Eyes and ears?*

I got out of bed, went into the living room, turned on the light, opened the Bible and it just fell open to "That is what the scriptures mean when they say 'No eye has seen, no ear has heard, and no mind has imagined what God has prepared for those who love him" (1 Corinthians 2:9 NLT). It was in this manner that God began to teach me. He would wake me at night and tell me many things. Not only that, it was also God who increased my reading skills—with the Bible.

So then it was, the King James Bible my husband had bought me years earlier became my ever-constant companion. I started reading it nonstop! I had an insatiable hunger for the Word of God. Don't tell me God can't give us understanding of his Word—I would cry so much because I understood this was a love letter to me! I needed to read so I could learn who I really was as a Christian.

Funny thing though, because I thought all Christians had this same thing going on in their lives. I was so happy and excited and just wanted to run and tell everyone what I was seeing, reading, and dreaming, But I quickly became surprised that not everyone wanted to hear. So I told Susie and my pastor all that was going on. They were happy for me and would have discussions with me explaining further what this new life in Christ was all about.

A Lifelong Friend

Not much later I met a lady named Nancy, and our first meeting was not particularly friendly. Not only had she and her family just started going to the same church I was attending, she also lived right across the street from me in the same house Marilyn had recently moved out of! (Marilyn had been instrumental in leading me to Jesus.) It was no accident and I was determined to meet Nancy. Even though one of her daughters told me that her mother thought I was weird, I pressed harder to get to know her.

Much like Marilyn had been with me, I, too, witnessed to Nancy all the time. I continually told her how great God was and all the incredible things he was doing in my life. My excitement could not be contained. And like I had previously acted around Marilyn, Nancy tried to avoid me! I just would not stop talking about God. I had become a "Marilyn" in Nancy's life.

But before too long, Nancy and I did become friends. And so it was, one day she and her husband were returning from a shopping trip at the local mall when Nancy told her husband, "I have to go to Dana's house." She called first and said she was supposed to come by.

As Nancy came into my house, she quickly explained that she did not know why she was there but that I had to pray for her. She also explained she just wanted to know if God was real, if all the great things I had been telling her for the past several days were real. I laid hands on Nancy and prayed with her, then told her to go home and read Jeremiah 33:3 which says, "Ask me and I will tell you remarkable secrets you do not know about things to come."

―❦―

When Nancy returned home, she read that passage but was also led to read John 14:14, "If ye shall ask any thing in my name, I will do it" (KJV). *Alright,* she thought and spontaneously lifted her hands and started speaking in tongues! Such was the flow she could not stop the tongues which poured out for hours! Nancy has never lost that fervor!

What's so beautiful about this experience with Nancy is that I had just read Acts chapter 2 in the Bible about the laying on of hands. Believe and receive! What a miracle. The thing is, I truly believed what I read in the Bible was for me. It was child-like faith. Nancy believed this way, too. She and I would read the Bible, then get on our faces and pray for hours wanting what we read! What a dear, faithful friend. I talk to Nancy often, even though we now live in different states, and we have been close friends for more than thirty years.

Nancy and I just grew and grew in the Lord during this time at each other's houses and at that little church in Texas where we met. Several times a year this church would host special speakers. One night, a particular guest speaker was praying and laying hands on people. He called me to the front to speak over me. Well, I wanted and was expecting for him to impart the gift of healing (that is laying hands on the sick) and the gift of prophecy—what I thought were the great gifts. As he laid his hands on me though, he said I had the gift of love. I said, "What?" He then said, "I've never seen this before, the spirit of love."

God proceeded to touch my heart and that night he filled me head to toe with his love. I did not know what a great gift this was—indeed, this was the greatest gift of all. It was years later that I understood how powerful God's kind of love is!

Enemy Attack

With all the great things happening in my life, after a while darkness came. Sometimes when I would take afternoon naps or be asleep at night when Gene, my husband, was not at home, something heavy like rubber would lay on me. Because this "thing" would hold my mouth closed, I couldn't scream. I couldn't do anything when this would happen to me for it exerted such pressure on my chest and my body as to hold me motionless. Now this thing was not visible nor discernable, except that it was evil.

When this would occur, which was oddly almost always during the day and was increasing in frequency, I kept asking God in my mind to help me. Again, I could not utter a sound with the weight of this thing on me, so in my mind I would ask, "God, what do I do? I pray; I resist; but this thing is still tormenting me." God would reply, "Say 'the blood.'" I would repeat, "the blood of Jesus," in my thoughts and the thing would leave. Afterwards, however, I would be completely drained of energy.

Even though this thing visited many times, I never told anyone, feeling too embarrassed to tell them that during these horrible times, a heaviness was holding me down and it felt like sexual abuse.

It was during this same time, I was being so used of God traveling and speaking in churches, that I just could not admit I was going through this awful occurrence. Not me, born again and so free. Pride would not let me tell of it. But one day after church, some ladies and I were talking. Somehow during the course of conversation, I brought up this mysterious matter and one of the ladies said she had experienced the same thing!

Enemy Spirit Identified

I continued to pray often that God would show me what this thing was. Then one day on television, it just so happened the word "incubus" appeared on the screen. Because of the nature of the TV program, I was prompted to look in the dictionary at this strange word.

It turns out, this tormenting spirit that visited me many times is called an incubus spirit! Webster's Dictionary defines it as "an evil spirit that lies on people in their sleep; one that has sexual intercourse with women while they're sleeping; one that oppresses or burdens like a nightmare." A nightmare indeed! Webster's Dictionary also defines nightmare as "an evil spirit formerly thought to oppress people during sleep; a frightening dream accompanied by a sense of oppression or suffocation that awakens the sleeper; a feeling of anxiety or terror."

Wow. When I read that definition, I knew how Satan was trying to bring the past to me again. But you know what? I had not truly let go of the past either. What I mean is, I had yet to forgive my father.

But one day as this invasive presence continued to visit me, Nancy called knowing something was wrong. I finally told her about this invading spirit and she came right over, anointed me with oil, and rebuked the incubus spirit. Nancy and I were still so new to faith in God, but we got our Bibles and started reading.

The Bible told us God was our Helper in time of need, so we turned to him in this time of great need. The Bible also told us, "Behold, I give unto you power to tread on serpents and scorpions, and over all the power of the enemy: and nothing shall by any means hurt you" (Luke 10:19 KJV). "And ye shall know the truth, and the truth shall make you free" (John 8:32 KJV). We knew to speak the Word of God out loud until we got free from this spirit.

We prayed, "Father, your ears are open to our cry. You said if any two agree, we shall ask, in the name of Jesus, and it shall be done. As the Bible says, 'Again I say unto you, That if two of you shall agree on earth as touching any thing that they shall ask, it shall be done for them of my Father which is in heaven. For where two or three are gathered together in my name, there am I in the midst of them'" (Matthew 18:19-20 KJV). We continued to pray, "we believe, Lord Jesus, that according to your Word the devil has come to steal, kill, and destroy. But God has come to give us life more abundantly (see John 10:10) and that you will never leave us nor forsake us" (see Hebrews 13:5).

After that time of prayer, that evil presence visited one more time and I had had enough. Nancy came, put my Bible on my chest, I made a line with my foot, and told the devil to come on. I had the Word of God in my mouth, the anointing of the Holy Spirit, and bless God, I won that battle once and for all. That evil spirit never returned.

Forgiving Pete

Now all through the years of being born again and during my times of reading the Bible, God would show me scriptures concerning forgiveness. Plus, I would even purposefully look up and spend time reading Bible verses about forgiveness. I knew it was a Bible command for Christians to forgive those who have wronged us and I deeply grieved over my father's misconduct. While doing this, conviction and prompting to forgive him would come but I just could not pardon my father's abusive, ruinous behavior toward me. Howbeit, holding onto unforgiveness was a serious weight to carry because it turned into bitterness and resentment. Yes, Pete had broken the law and served time; but wasn't I breaking God's law, too?

After much study of the Bible and struggle within myself, the day finally came when I said in my heart, *I forgive my father.* Not long after my decision to forgive, I was asleep on the sofa and awakened for some odd reason. A vision promptly came in which I saw God holding my father in one of his arms and me in the other. I then saw God look at Pete and heard him say, "I forgive him." Next, God looked at me and said, "Now you forgive him."

I fell on my face and oh, such crying and travailing deep within me occurred as all the years of anger, pain, and hatred were released to be replaced with an amazing love and forgiveness for my father. Tears of forgiveness cleansed me from all the things that were residing deep in my heart and love that I had never had for my father filled me. "Since God chose you to be the holy people he loves, you must clothe yourselves with tenderhearted mercy, kindness, humility, gentleness, and patience" (Colossians 3:12 NLT).

Because my half-sister, Helen, occasionally stayed in touch with me over the years, through her I knew where my father lived and had his phone number. After God showed me that vision of forgiveness, the time soon came when I called Pete and told him I forgave him. He listened respectfully as I also explained that I was born again and told him all about my wonderful, new life with God and that I desired he have this new kind of life. I explained salvation to him then mailed him a Bible and salvation literature along with a letter I had written.

Meanwhile, one Wednesday night at church with my family, I was tapped on the shoulder and told I had a phone call. Helen had called to inform me that Pete had died from a heart attack. My husband and I drove to Houston, Texas, for the funeral but along the way, I prayed that God would somehow show me that Pete had received Christ before he died. When we arrived at his house, I went into his bedroom and on the headboard of his bed was the salvation literature I had sent and an open Bible! Praise the Lord!

I truly believe anyone, no matter who or under what circumstance, can get born again by asking Christ into their heart. God made the way to himself simple. "If you confess with your mouth that Jesus is Lord and believe in your heart that God raised him from the dead, you will be saved. For it is by believing in your heart that you are made right with God, and it is by confessing with your mouth that you are saved. . . . For 'everyone who calls on the name of the Lord will be saved'" (Romans 10:9-10,13 NLT).

The Bible teaches much about salvation and forgiveness, faith and love, but also about the consequences of sin. I know that all the anger, hate, and unforgiveness I had in my heart was not any different from the incest my father committed. Without Jesus, we would all be lost and separated from God eternally.

People would always angrily ask me how could I forgive such an offender as my father. How could I forgive such abuse and misuse? That man wrecked my life, how could I pardon him? My reply would always be, "Jesus Christ forgave me. I just have to do the same." I never argue nor debate. I explain it is only by the transforming power of the Word of God and prayer and that even though it took time and I fought for it, forgiveness is one of the most liberating things a Christian can and must do.

"But I say unto you, 'Love your enemies, bless them that curse you, do good to them that hate you, and pray for them which despitefully use you, and persecute you'" (Matthew 5:44 KJV). The Bible tells us to walk in love towards the people who abuse us, abandon us, or hurt us. That is obeying God's word and walking in Jesus' love the way He loves us.

The most amazing part of this was that my father asked Jesus into his heart a short time after I called to tell him that I forgave him. That occurred right before he died of a massive heart attack at the age of 58. And I can truly say I know I will see him in heaven.

A Glorious Reunion

The miraculous events were to continue. The year was 1984. One particular morning on Mother's Day while I was in church, the pastor asked all mothers and their daughters to come to the front for celebration and prayer. While watching them assemble at the front, I immediately became distraught and felt intense pain at not being able to know the joy those women had.

Despite the knowledge that my mother did not want me, had abandoned me, and was absent my entire life, at age 37, I still had a strong desire to meet her. Where was she? What was she like? I wished she was near. That Mother's Day the desire consumed me and I prayed, "God, what about my mother? I would just love to know who my mother is."

It turns out later at home, I remembered having received a piece of crumpled, torn paper when Pete died with my birth information on it. It said "unnamed baby girl, mother's name Mary Ann Cervantes, Coconino County, Flagstaff." I also recalled during my years at the children's home after Pete's arrest, that every now and then I would somehow hear the name "Cervantes" spoken. It did not make sense to me then. Perhaps during the time of his arrest and trial, Pete had told the police the true name of my mother. I also remembered Pete telling me early on that my mother was a no-good person and not to think about her. Nevertheless, like a jigsaw puzzle, the pieces of my past life were about to fit together.

I quickly dialed the telephone operator and asked for the number of "Mary Ann Cervantes." The operator replied, "Ma'am, there are lots of people with the last name Cervantes, but I will give you one of the numbers and just maybe they will know her." I jotted down the number and hung up.

That night after church, I returned home and dialed that number. (It was still Mother's Day.) A young girl answered the phone and I asked, "Does a Mary Ann Cervantes live there?" The little girl called out, "Grandma, someone wants to talk to you." A voice then said, "Hello." I cheerfully replied, "Happy Mother's Day!" "Who are you?" she inquired. I responded, "Did you have a daughter 37 years ago?" and told her my father's name. She instantly burst into tears, which caused me to burst into tears, and for all the joyful crying, we could no longer talk! This was my mother whom I had never seen, but had always yearned to meet someday. Talk about an answer to prayer—just that morning at church! I could not believe the joy I felt!

Unexpected Blessings

My mother and I proceeded to get acquainted through several phone conversations over a short period of time. To this day though, I do not know how news of reuniting with my mother traveled so fast. Just days after meeting my mother by phone, I was at my desk at work when a paid-in-full, round trip airplane ticket to Flagstaff, Arizona, was delivered to me! At long last, I was going to meet my mother!

Overjoyed, I also wanted a traveling companion to make this momentous trip with me. My husband could not get away from his work and Brent, my older son, was committed to playing in a football game. Therefore my younger son,

Brad, who was then about 12 years old, accompanied me, also with a paid-in-full airline ticket provided anonymously.

As we landed in Arizona, I was becoming more nervous and excited that this meeting was actually happening. I could hardly sit still and had a flock of butterflies in my stomach. Upon arriving at the Flagstaff airport, I called a taxi to take my son and I to my mother's house. The taxi driver was most friendly and helpful and in simply making conversation asked, "What brings you to Arizona?" I answered, "This is just nothing but a miracle," and briefly told him how I found my mother on Mother's Day and that we were about to meet for the first time since I was born.

While listening to my story, the driver started crying and asked if his wife who worked for the local newspaper could meet us, write a story, and take pictures to be published in the paper. I politely declined because of potentially putting my mother in an awkward position of not yet having met me. Besides, this moment was so important, almost sacred, that I thought it should be kept private until we knew each other better. (However, it was not long after our initial meeting that an article and photograph was published in a local magazine in the town where I resided in Texas.)

Another reason I declined the publicity was that previously during our second phone conversation, my mother informed me I had a half-brother and sister but that she had never once mentioned I had been born. She now had to tell them about me! My half-brother, whom I eventually met, was excited to meet me; my half-sister was not ready to. Knowing that, it was better the public did not yet know about this miraculous family reunion.

A Long-Awaited Meeting

The special moment, anticipated for a lifetime, finally arrived. As the taxi pulled up to my mother's house, the driver exclaimed, "We're here!" But prior to arriving at the house, I had mentioned to the driver that the company I worked for in Pampa, Texas, had also given me a camera for this special trip and would he take a picture for me to keep for myself. He replied, "Of course!"

My mother was waiting on her front porch with a close friend of hers and the friend's daughter. As soon as mother saw me get out of the taxi along with my son, she left the porch and came towards us. We instantly embraced each other long and hard, and in doing so, I smelled cologne. It was the very same cologne I had worn for years. Imagine that! I told her that was my cologne of choice and she said that was the only one she ever wore. Not only did we have that in common, many other similarities were discovered as the night wore on.

Later that evening, my mother and I, as well as the friend and daughter were sitting around the kitchen table after enjoying dinner together. Mother's friend loved on me as much as if I were her missing daughter coming home. The conversation eventually led to my mother wanting to know all about me. I told her everything from Pete taking me away at the age of 5, to the incestuous behavior and extreme isolation, to the chain of events that led to his arrest, to my difficult years at the children's home and at school, up to my marriage to a wonderful man and our two sons.

During the course of me recounting my eventful life story, everyone at that kitchen table was crying—everyone except Brad who was not present, for he was in another part of the house watching television. However, I found it a little odd that the teenaged daughter was upset and crying at hearing my life story. It was not until later that evening I found out why.

But before that, yet another oddity became evident. Throughout our conversation, I became more and more amazed how very much like my absentee mother I was. Besides the identical cologne we preferred, we chose similar clothing styles of bright colors. Plus, we both belonged to the same kind of Pentecostal church. We both loved to be hospitable by always preparing large of amounts of food, ever ready to serve the numerous people who would randomly drop by.

And of greater importance, we both individually became born again close to the same time and upon similar kinds of circumstance. My mother had had so much guilt and shame for abandoning me and for the path in life which she took, that she too had suicidal intentions that were intervened by the loving God of the Bible! She chose to live, not die, by calling out to him and got born again like I did.

Another Momentous Event

Mother's friends soon left, for we were all worn out from the day's heart-stirring conversation. I finally got into bed only to be awakened by mother a short time later. It was 1:30 a.m. Strangely, she could not say my name the entire time I was there, but simply called me, "Hon." "Hon, wake up. I need you to come into the den." Sleepily, I crawled out of bed and followed my mother not knowing what to expect.

The same lady and her teenaged daughter who were present earlier that day and throughout that evening were sitting in the den. They looked quite distressed and both were virtually wailing. I quickly thought back at how the daughter had cried when I was telling my life story previously at the kitchen table.

It turns out the young girl had only just informed her mother for the first time on their way home that evening, that her father was doing the same to her. Her father was molesting her sexually and no one knew it! She was able to tell her story to me as it came pouring out of her like a swiftly moving river and when she finished, the first thing I did was to ask if she wanted to know Jesus. "Yes," she answered promptly and we prayed for her salvation and then we prayed again, this time for wisdom for her and her mother.

After a few priceless days in my mother's house, the time came when I had to return home. But by telling my story on that first day, I allowed other people into a dark secret, which then paved the way for another victim of the same kind of abuse to find a way out—a way out of the shame, guilt, and despair through Jesus Christ. This just proves we never know when God has someone that needs our testimony.

I have since had so many women tell me that they came from a Christian home with great parents and they felt like they had no testimony. Wow! How blessed they are to be able to say that. But, they need to know they still have a walk with God that's worth telling a hurting world. They do have a testimony of how faithful God is day by day throughout their lifetime no matter what!

I was most fortunate to have visited my mother in Flagstaff when I did and to see her one more time, because within a year of initially meeting her, she died from health problems. Yes, I was saddened and it was a loss, but like my father's passing, I took comfort knowing I would see my mother again in heaven.

Resting in Him

As I tell this story today, I feel so blessed because we do not know how our lives are going to be a blessing to someone later! I know that I have a blessed walk with Jesus. It may be hard to put into words, but to know Jesus the way I do is so wonderful.

To have been broken, abused, and fearful, and yet God would put a scripture in the Bible for me, "Even if my father and mother abandon me, the Lord will hold me close" (Psalm 27:10 NLT). When my father and mother forsake me, then the Lord will take me up. He will gather me up. *Wow!* That is why I started calling Jesus my Daddy. "He will feed his flock like a shepherd. He will carry the lambs in his arms, holding them close to his heart" (Isaiah 40:11a NLT).

Relax in his everlasting arms. The eternal God is your refuge and underneath are his everlasting arms. God is so aware of you that when you are weak he is strong. Let him carry you when you have no energy.

God would say to you today, "Rest in me. Refresh yourself in my presence." Let go of cares and worries so that you can receive his peace. Open your heart and mind to receive all he has for you.

God wants you to talk to him about your struggles, your fears, your family, or your sickness. Just be honest and tell him you are in pain, not understanding what to do. He loves when you empty yourself and let him in to fill you with his peace, his comfort, and the knowledge that all is well.

PART TWO

Living in His Light

I am the light of the world: He that followeth me shall not walk in darkness, but shall have the light of life.

—John 8:12

My Life Today

I have had the honor of speaking and teaching in church services, including prayer meetings and women's meetings, in numerous churches throughout Texas, Oklahoma, Missouri, and Louisiana. During these times I have witnessed many salvations and healings in people of all ages. God has used my life story to testify of his amazing grace and unconditional love.

Since being born again, I have always ministered to anyone about Jesus and have loved sharing my story of having been abandoned and forsaken, but not forgotten by God! Everyone needs to know that God loves them right now and that he has wonderful things to give them. He has salvation and healing and deliverance and peace to give! "Don't be afraid! Speak out! Don't be silent! For I am with you, and no one will attack and harm you, for many people here in this city belong to me" (Acts 18:9-10 NLT).

Also, as miraculous as was being taught to read by God with the Bible, so was being trained by him to become a massage therapist as a ministry unto him. Many people came to me over several years for relaxation or pain relief in their bodies. Ministers and church leaders as well as people from all walks of life came for my services. I was able to tell my story to numerous clients and listen to theirs which paved the way for personal ministry and prayer.

Another significant experience in my life was that of being interviewed on *The 700 Club* with Pat Robertson. God had previously told me I would tell my story on television one day and that a book would be written. It was truly God who opened the way for my TV appearance and now a book has been written! Watching this happen absolutely shows that God directs our steps for his higher purposes. If he says it, he will do it!

After retiring from massage therapy, I learned to play golf with my husband. My older son, Brent, as you may remember from my story, is a pro golfer and my younger son, Brad, enjoys playing, too. I just love the sport and being with my guys, but the places it takes me and the people I meet are wonderful opportunities to speak about God.

Always, always someone needs to hear about Jesus. God knows just who to place in our path for us to talk about him! Be ready and watchful for those open doors to tell of God's goodness and love.

God is continually showing me how faithful he is. I have seen his promises coming alive daily since I asked him into my heart. If I've learned anything these past several years, it's this: not to worry about one thing! Not to worry about myself, my family, anything! I am free from trying and from wasting time worrying. God is trustworthy and able.

God does teach us such simple ways and things. One time, my husband took one of our grandsons, Nick, fishing. Nick was three years old at the time and had a hard time releasing the fishing line. My husband kept saying, "Release it, Nick." He was really struggling with what he heard his Papa say, not knowing what he was releasing. He stood nearby watching his Papa and all at once Nick said, "Oh, Papa, I get it. Let it go!" Three years old and he understood it. God, please teach us the way you did with Nick, to let go of anything we do not understand.

That is what God wants us to do. Watch *him* until we learn to let it go. Let go of all the things that worry us and that seem troublesome or difficult to understand. When we let go, God can then take care of it.

I thank God for my wonderful husband, Gene, and that we have been married more than 45 years. We raised two fine boys who have their own beautiful families and who are all born again. Even though I had many problems during our early years of marriage, Gene had grace to stay with me. He also had God's favor to be able to understand me when I didn't. God blessed my husband, for when I was not lovable he loved me!

I also want to mention that I had the ultimate privilege of leading my three grandsons to the Lord when they were around 5 and 6 years old by telling them how much Jesus loved them. I cannot think of anything else that could make me happier! Nick, Cade, and Jace all walk in so much love and are full of the Lord. What an eternal joy to my heart! God will show himself to you today. Believe and receive it. I pray this for you. God bless you.

Becoming Born Again

"For I was born a sinner—yes, from the moment my mother conceived me" (Psalm 51:5). We all have to be born again!

I pray that as you read my story you see your need for a savior—the Savior Jesus Christ. All anyone has to do is "Confess with your mouth that Jesus is Lord and believe in your heart that God raised Him from the dead, you will be saved. . . . For anyone who calls on the name of the Lord will be saved" (Romans 10:9,13).

Jesus tells us he stands at the door of our heart and knocks. "Look! Here I stand at the door and knock. If you hear me calling and open the door, I come in, and we will share a meal as friends" (Revelation 3:20). We are instantly in the family of God when we ask him into our hearts. Jesus also tells us, "I give them eternal life, and they will never perish. No one will snatch them away from me, for my Father has given them to me, and he is more powerful than anyone else. So no one can take them from me" (John 10:28-29).

The most important thing you do after praying and asking Jesus in your heart is to get a Bible and the Holy Spirit will teach you all about his wisdom and knowledge. We need to grow in him. Reverent fear of the Lord is the foundation of true wisdom. All who obey his commandments will grow in wisdom. "Reverence for the Lord is the foundation of true wisdom. The rewards of wisdom come to all who obey him, Praise his name forever," (Psalm 111:10).

The Kingdom of God is entered only by the new birth. "What this means is that those who become Christians become new persons. They are not the same anymore, for the old life is gone. A new life has begun!" (2 Corinthians 5:17). Wow, that is straight from God's mouth to us because we accepted him as our Lord Jesus Christ!

"All this newness of life is from God, who brought us back to himself through what Christ did. And God has given us the task of reconciling people to him. For God was in Christ, reconciling the world to himself, no longer counting people's sins against them. This is the wonderful message he has given us to tell others" (2 Corinthians 5:18-19).

I did not even know that I was doing this when I was born again, but I wanted to tell everyone about this great feeling I had! I knew after I came out of my bedroom in 1978 that I was different, and when you become born again, you will also know your heart feels so much better.

"For it was I, the Lord your God, who rescued you from the land of Egypt. Open your mouth wide, and I will fill it with good things" (Psalm 81:10). God promises that if we seek him, he will fill our mouths with the words we need to say.

If you made the decision to ask Jesus into your heart, he is in you now and you in him. May the God of hope fill you with joy and peace. Believe that he loves you and understands you completely.

Come to God with a teachable spirit, for he communicates through his spirit to yours and through his word. It's only by God's Holy Spirit that you can and will be changed into his glory. You are fearfully and wonderfully made for such a time as this.

My greatest prayer is for the salvation of others, for broken hearts and wounded souls to be healed in Jesus' name. He loves you so much. What he has done for me, he will do for you. I pray God's favor to you that you will want to be set free to love God and everyone else. *It is real.*

Growing with God

God and I have a love affair. I love God with all my heart. I knew I was a new person when I was born again. Everything was bright and I loved my family so much. Never had I felt this way. I loved going to that first church and could not wait to hear what God had to say. The pastor was so full of love and let us all know how much God loved us. The church had lots of singing guests and guest speakers, which made it different to watch and to see how God was so real. Thank God for the foundation I got upon becoming a new Christian!

I can remember when I was first born again, I would take my boys to school and could not wait to return home to read the Bible. I *wanted* everything God said I could have! I just believed the Bible. Every word was like Jesus teaching me and talking to me. I was so in love with Jesus. I remember reading and seeing Jesus and the disciples walking and could almost smell the dust! The Bible was so full of life and made me so happy. I felt God's presence when I would read and talk to him. I love Jesus so much.

God has done so much for my thoughts, heart, and mind upon becoming born again and because God's Spirit came on me, I can say I have not been the same. His word sounds like he is reading to me, as I cry. I have such a desire for God's Word to come alive in me, because I love the Word of God and want to ask people if they really know Jesus. I feel what I read and I pray that you experience this same love.

It has been years since I was born again, but it just gets better and better every day with the Lord in my life. God says if we stay close to him, he is the way. He will guide us along today's journey. We have to enjoy today, right now, and not worry about what is around the corner. Concentrate on enjoying life right now. We are on the path God has chosen for us right this moment. Rest in Jesus and trust him for everything. He is our tomorrow also; we can rest in knowing that.

Being in the Presence of God

When I was first born again I prayed a lot and when I prayed in the spirit, it was as though I was sitting at Jesus' feet. I felt his presence. I would see and hear things that would make me so happy. Then after the conversation or visit with Jesus, I would not be able to describe what I heard or saw, but it was the greatest thing. Afterwards, for hours or days, I felt differently—nothing bothered me, just peace and joy were with me. I have experienced this many times in my life.

"To those who are open to my teaching, more understanding will be given" (Mark 4:25a). We have to decide to start reading the Bible today. I know that when I picked up the Bible for the first time, God gave me such a hunger to know him. How else do we find out who our Creator is? The Bible is full of life. I pray that the anointing of the Holy Ghost will also cause you to want to draw close to him.

God does speak to us; we have to know his voice. The Bible is a teaching manual to know Jesus and all he has for us. When we do not have a lot of stuff in our head, it becomes easy to read the Word of God and to believe it. "As your words are taught, they give light, even the simple can understand them" (Psalm 119:130).

Wisdom Speaks

After becoming born again, I have developed a holy boldness in me. I truly feel I can be me. I am not out to please anyone but Jesus Christ. He says he will even make my enemies silent. My desire has been to speak the truth and not to be afraid of what someone may think of me. I am no longer a people pleaser.

"For I speak the truth and hate every kind of deception. My advice is wholesome and good. There is nothing crooked or twisted in it. My words are plain to anyone with understanding, clear to those who want to learn" (Proverbs 8:7-9). Desire to speak the truth of God's Word into yourself and know that his Word is life to you.

"Leave your foolish ways behind, and begin to live; learn how to be wise" (Proverbs 9:6). The book of Proverbs teaches us how to live and how to have an abundance from each word of wisdom written there. Oh God, that we your children will hunger for the real things of this time here in life. "Getting wisdom is the most important thing you can do! And whatever else you do, get good judgment" (Proverbs 4:7).

Place Your Hope in God

Sick people without hope will receive hope. People will receive God's love like never before. They will receive joy, peace, and understanding of God and his Word. They will receive healing and deliverance and people will be set free from abuse!

There is hope. There is hope for children. There is hope for finances. There is hope for friendships. There is hope for mates. There is hope that you will come out of darkness into the marvelous light of Jesus Christ.

Hope is something positive we have had since childhood. But the kind of hope I had was that my dad would not make me stay awake at night for him, that he would not treat me the way he did. I was always hoping my life would be different.

Then while living in the children's home, I just hoped my father would not come to visit because I knew what he would do to me even with my sister, Helen, being there! He would sneak in to do things to me, all the while I was hoping someday he would never touch me again.

In the meantime, I was hoping to get married and have someone protect me from my father. This hope became realized and I thank God for the wonderful man who later became my husband and who made sure my father could not come around after we were married. My husband is a blessing to me. Even though we married at a young age, we have stayed married for more than 45 years. And even though we started our lives together with little, my husband, being such a hard worker, has been a consistent provider, protector, and proud father of our two sons, I have been so blessed with blessings still coming to me and my family.

Hope comes from reading this wonderful letter to us, the Bible, saying take heart because we have peace in Jesus. "I have told you all this so that you may have peace in me. Here on earth you will have many trials and sorrows. But take heart, because I have overcome the world" (John 16:33).

I know you may be in the middle of trials and sorrows. I speak peace over you and pray that you draw peace from Jesus. He says to come to him when you are hurting and he will take your pain. Let go of cares while Jesus changes your heart and your mind. Let go of worries and take the peace Jesus freely gives. Take time to hear his voice and that is especially through the Word of God. The book of Proverbs is wonderful for growing and knowing who we are and who our Savior is.

"In the same way, wisdom is sweet to your soul. If you find it, you will have a bright future, and your hopes will not be cut short" (Proverbs 24:14). When you have been disappointed, praise God, for these words are of a bright future. There is always hope.

A Picture of Me in His Hand

One day while just thinking, I considered how most people have baby pictures of themselves. Most people also have a valid birth certificate which in turn helps them acquire other legal documents in life, such as a Visa to travel to foreign countries. But I have none of these things.

These people also have childhood memories. I really do not have a single remembrance of a Christmas celebration or any other holiday of any kind. I have no fond childhood stories to tell, I have no special childhood memories to reflect on. I listen to friends tell about trips that their family went on when they were children or some very special gift they got for some reason. So as I am thinking about this I cry! The reason I am crying is I believe in my heart that is why I have such a special walk with my heavenly Father.

Maybe I have no memories; maybe I have no pictures, but I know without a doubt, my picture is in the palm of Jesus' hand. Every time he looks at his hands, he sees me. Never to be forgotten. Never to be forsaken. Pictures fade and pictures get lost, but I see that my heavenly Father carries my picture with him everywhere—never to be lost! Praise the Lord.

"As for me, I am poor and needy, but the Lord is thinking about me right now. You are my helper and my savior. Do not delay, O my God" (Psalm 40:17). The Lord is thinking of me right now and the Holy Spirit said that he was the greatest gift I could ever receive. What a blessing to hear this from *God!*

Boldness

The Holy Spirit is so in love with us. Different people are telling how they are praying more and spending time reading their Bibles. It seems like God is showing up big in their lives. A change can be seen like people rising up and praying in public, talking about miracles in their lives, or testimonies of family and friends. It is an awareness that we are talking openly about God. This was not seen like it is now. God is getting the praise he so deserves.

I can speak for myself! From the moment of being born again, I have always loved Jesus. I could always talk about the things of the Lord with my friends. Even now, it is as easy as breathing for me to talk and tell people what God is doing in my life. With freedom, there is so much joy. Excitement is meant to share and not be hidden because I was ashamed or afraid I would lose a friend.

I see things changing so fast in the news. What a great thing it is to tell someone there is a God who will help them during this time of trial and tribulation in our country. It is so easy to tell them to call on Jesus to save them and he will be their counselor.

Made a Witness and a Minister of the Lord

Several years ago, a friend from a church in Texas called and said God told her that Acts 26:16-18 was what I would be speaking someday. Someday is here now! Glory to God. "But rise and stand upon thy feet: for I have appeared unto thee for this purpose, to make thee a minister and a witness both of these things which thou hast seen, and of those things in the which I will appear unto thee; delivering thee from the people, and from the Gentiles, unto whom now I send thee, to open their eyes, and to turn them from darkness to light, and the power of Satan unto God, that they may receive forgiveness of sins, and inheritance among them which are sanctified by faith that is in me" (KJV).

I have also learned when we pray about something, we have to believe God's Word no matter what. I have found in many years as a Christian, sometimes it will take years to see things come to pass. Trust and believe. Without faith it is impossible to believe.

It can be a slow walk when we are born again, but I am so excited to have come from a horrible life and then to know that I am just as clean as the Apostles Peter, John, Mark, and even Jesus himself. It is very exciting that God makes this so simple to the simple people. So thankful I was reading and believing.

Jesus Christ is God's love gift to the world (John 3:16). And believers are the Father's love gift to Jesus Christ. It is Christ who commits the believer to the Father for safe keeping, so that the believer's security rests upon the Father's faithfulness to his Son Jesus Christ.

"The Spirit of the Lord is upon me, for he has appointed me to preach Good News to the poor. He has sent me to proclaim that captives will be released, that the blind will see, that the downtrodden will be freed from their oppressors, and that the time of the Lord's favor has come" (Luke 4:18-19).

I Am Your Father God

One time while talking to the Father and praising him for my life, he said to my heart, "Suffering is but a fleeting moment." I can honestly say I thank God for all I've been through. That suffering now seems fleeting compared to what I currently have. But I love my walk with God more than life! I see how all the Word comes alive after reading and studying it for years. My heart is so full of God and his love.

For years I have written things down—things I felt the Holy Spirit was saying to me. They were love letters from him. I wasn't just thinking these things. It was the lover of my soul speaking to me. I know without a doubt it was God speaking. "Be silent, and know that I am God! I will be honored by every nation. I will be honored throughout the world" (Psalm 46:10). He would speak to my heart with his Word and I would write it on paper and date the times this would happen.

"My sheep recognize my voice; I know them, and they follow me" (John 10:27). I believe that he speaks to those who have ears to hear. All these beautiful words from my heavenly Father have changed my heart! I know we can't obey feelings. But my heart and thoughts have lined up with what God says. The Word of God is beautiful and helps daily with the things ahead. The Holy Spirit does speak to us.

Many, many times I have taken my needs to my Father. "You will live in joy and be led forth in peace. The mountains and hills will burst into song, and the trees of the field will clap their hands!" (Isaiah 55:12). We will go out in joy and be led forth in peace. That is where our strength comes from, not from things or people.

The Power of Words

About 10 years ago, a friend from another state came to visit me for the weekend. Our first night together, she was sharing her testimony and that of her husband's. I had never heard anything like it. I even got up and got a towel I was crying so hard. God had done such a healing in both her and her husband's lives from years of heartaches. I went to bed that night with such joy and peace.

The next night this same friend and I were talking again about the same things. However, I noticed this time it was different; now her tone was anger. The first night she had been praising her husband, the second night she was filled with anger about her husband. While stunned at her change in tone of voice, I looked up and in the spirit I saw Satan in the corner of the room giving orders to a demon to go to her husband and torment him during the night. Because of my friend's angry words toward her husband, I saw demon spirits just ready to shoot out the door at Satan's command! We learned a great lesson that night.

"Death and life are in the power of the tongue: and they that great it shall eat the fruit thereof" (Proverbs 18:21 KJV).

Tears

I have been crying so much since I have come into this new level I am in. One night I was crying while praying and talking to Jesus. Cry, cry, cry. I cry when I'm happy; I cry when I pray. I asked God one time what I was doing, why all the crying, He told me he bottles every tear I cry—and everyone else's for that matter. He has every tear that ever spilled from our eyes! Then he showed me large rain barrels. One after another lined up. I laughed!

Another time I asked him again why all the crying. I happened to have my TV on a Christian broadcasting channel. A pastor that was speaking at that particular moment said that someone was crying a lot and that it was a language only God understood. So let my tears come, Lord Jesus! I will never be ashamed of my tears. There were so many years I could not cry. Now, I cry freely. But then, my own name fits me to a tee—Dana Cryer!

PART THREE

Inspirations from God

Your word is a lamp to my feet and a light to my path.

—Psalms 119:105

We are Special in Daddy's Eyes

We are so blessed to have a God that listens to our heart. It is the greatest feeling to be able to talk to him anytime about everything. And that is why we have the joy of the Lord. Our trust is in our Father God!

"He made their hearts, so he understands everything they do" (Psalm 33:15).

"Taste and see that the Lord is good. Oh, the joys of those who trust in him!" (Psalm 34:8).

"I rise early, before the sun is up; I cry out for help and put my hope in your words. I stay awake through the night, thinking about your promise" (Psalm 119:147-148).

We are special in our heavenly Daddy's eyes. He has a living Word for us to follow and he has given us hearts to understand. We ask for help—our help is in the Word. God's promises are true. Get into his Word to live a victorious life. God has revealed to us the truth there.

"And now, just as you accepted Christ Jesus as your Lord, you must continue to live in obedience to him, Let your roots grow down into him and draw up nourishment from him so you will grow in faith, strong and vigorous in the truth you were taught, Let your lives overflow with thanksgiving for all he has done" (Colossians 2:6-7). This is the new life in Christ.

"May God our Father give you grace and peace" (Colossians 1:2b).

"Surely goodness and mercy shall follow me all the days of my life: and I will dwell in the house of the Lord forever" (Psalm 23:6 KJV).

Having a New Home, a New Heart

God, thank you for your Word. We pray to live holy as you are in our lives. We want to be just like Jesus and have a home like our home above. We want to be holy in our conversations and attitudes. Just like packing our suitcase for a trip, we want clean things in the suitcase (in our heart). We want pure and holy thoughts there.

"So set yourselves apart to be holy, for I, the Lord am your God. Keep all my laws and obey them, for I am the Lord, who makes you holy" (Leviticus 20:7-8). God is holy. What is holy? Consecrated or set aside for sacred use; standing apart from sin and evil.

God loves us so much and we need his truth, which is the Word of God that sets us free. We become free by reading the Word and agreeing with it. We obey God's Word and sin will not entice us. If we do have sins, we can boldly enter into God's presence and receive forgiveness by confessing those sins. Confess means to admit or acknowledge our sin. Then, do not carry around the weight of those sins after confessing to God. He said he never remembers them again. It is a new lease on life.

It is so good to confess our sins because then God refreshes us from his presence. There is nothing like knowing the refreshment from our heavenly Father. "But if we confess our sins to him, he is faithful and just to forgive us and to cleanse us from every wrong" (1 John 1:9).

For instance, when our children did something wrong, we knew it. We got them to talk about it, then sometimes they would be crying about it because of the fear of punishment. We talked to them, and then saw joy once they confessed and moved on. At that point, we could not even remember what they did! That is like our Father in heaven loving us so much that he remembers it no more. And nothing can separate us from God's love.

"What can we say about such wonderful things as these? If God is for us, who can ever be against us? Who dares accuse us whom God has chosen for his own? Will God? No! He is the one who has given right standing with himself. Who then will condemn us? Will Jesus Christ? No, for he is the one who died for us and was raised to life for us and is sitting at the place of highest honor next to God, pleading for us. Can anything ever separate us from Christ's love? Does it mean He no longer loves us if we have trouble or calamity or are persecuted or are hungry or cold or in danger or threatened with death?" (Romans 8:31,33-35).

Keep it Simple – Let it Go

"But I say, 'Love your enemies! Pray for those who persecute you'" (Matthew 5:44). Make your life easier by letting go! God will promote you, but not if you are angry, offended, or holding on to the past. Let it go!

God will help us that have been harmed or hurt. He will use this to make us stronger and use us for his glory. Trust and obey the Word and just see what God can do for you. God is so good! I would not change anything I've been through, just because I know my walk with God is so wonderful. *God loves us so much!*

Simply believe. Choose to believe what you read in the Bible! Prayer time is so important. When God speaks to us, love comes. Learn to love being with him. There is *nothing* like it!

Freedom to Obey God

Jesus loves us so much that his arms are open at all times. If we would just run to him when we know we have done wrong. "Don't you realize that whatever you choose to obey becomes your master?" (Romans 6:16).

"But you belong to God, my dear children. You have already won your fight with these false prophets, because the Spirit who lives in you is greater than the spirit who lives in the world" (1 John 4:4). Even though we live in a nation that is taking God out of everything it can such as money—In God We Trust; prayer—out of schools; marriage—disavow vows; we still have and always will have freedom to walk with and obey God.

The Word of God Changes Us!

Sometimes after reading the Word of God and praying about a scripture over and over we will be tested. For instance, we might be tempted to think on things that we know we should not. But still the most important thing we can do is read and pray every day to understand and speak the Word of God.

Spending time in the Word of God will get us to the point where thinking of something we shouldn't will bother our conscience. That is because God corrects us with his Word. If we expect to hear from God, we have to listen to his voice and we can hear from him by reading his Word.

God will put people in our lives that will speak the truth over us. For instance, I was doing something that I knew I shouldn't and the Holy Spirit would deal with me about it. I happened to be outside watering plants one day when a friend I hadn't seen in years drove by looking for my house. She realized she found me and stopped to give me a word from God that she had no idea I had been struggling with. She gave me scriptures which I knew came from God. I received that and wanted to make the necessary changes in my life.

But it can be hard to obey the Word of God when it convicts us of wrongs. The first thing that happens is that Satan tries to put guilt and shame on us in the areas where we don't pray or confess our faults. Then slowly we are not praying or reading the Word at all, which causes us to slip slowly away from the truth. But God corrects his children, often with his Word, to help us come back to him.

"Everything that is now hidden or secret will eventually be brought to light. Anyone who is willing to hear should listen and understand! And be sure to pay attention to what you hear. The more you do this, the more you will understand—and even more besides" (Mark 4:22-24).

Abandonment

"For he hath said, 'I will never leave thee nor forsake thee'" (Hebrews 13:5).

"The Lord will not abandon his chosen people, for that would dishonor his great name, He made you a special nation for himself" (1 Samuel 12:22).

"Even if my father and my mother abandon me, the LORD will hold me close" (Psalm 27:10).

"No, I will not abandon you as orphans—I will come to you" (John 14:18).

After you have received Christ as your Savior, know that he will take the place of all those things stolen from you. Jesus says he is the abundance! Every need and care we have is where he wants to bless us with his peace and love.

As we grow in him, our desire is for things of God and to trust him for everything in our lives. He has his everlasting arms around us at all times. Relax and enjoy God's presence now in the present. Trust this, you will never be the same once you totally give your heart to Jesus Christ!

Rest in his presence when you need refreshment. Start reading the Bible and you will find a fresh word for every need you have. Be conscious of God and start thanking him for all his blessings, his love, his protection, his provisions. This requires time alone with him. Relax. Be still. And know that he is God! "Be still and know that I am God" (Psalm 46:10 KJV).

Living in the Light

"For he hath said, 'I will never leave thee, nor forsake thee'" (Hebrews 13:5b KJV). Just think about someone *never* leaving you. Never means not ever, at no time, not under any condition. Never leave means never to go away from, depart, desert, abandon, withdraw from. Never forsake means never to withdraw from or abandon.

What a comforting word from God himself to us his children, he will never leave us at any time, under any condition, even during surgery or watching TV or driving or with friends or playing sports. He will never abandon us. God is with us while we are sleeping and waking up. He is with us every morning and throughout our day. That is why it is so powerful to talk with the Lord when we wake up.

Take time to be quiet and listen to him talk about his written Word. Let Jesus direct your thoughts towards him. That is also why it's so important to know the promises of the Bible. Repeat what you know you should do, The Ten Commandments, for example, or The Lord's Prayer. (See Matthew 6:9-13.) Always aim that love will be your walk. God is love and says so much about love in the Bible.

We can also pray for God's help anytime. Pray with the psalmist. "I am determined not to sin in what I say" (Psalm 17:3b). But if we do say something wrong, God's Word rises up within us and we can correct it right then, not letting it take our joy.

"As your words are taught, they give light; even the simple can understand them. . . . Guide my steps by your word, so I will not be overcome by any evil" (Psalm 119:130,133).

God's Peace

God is with you and watches over you wherever you go. "The Lord is my strength, my shield from every danger. I trust in him with all my heart. He helps me, and my heart is filled with joy I burst out in songs of thanksgiving" (Psalm 28:7).

God says whenever you start to feel afraid, remember that he is your shield. His presence watches over you, continually protecting you from both known and unknown dangers. "God is our refuge and strength, always ready to help in times of trouble" (Psalm 46:1). The Lord watches over you. "You know when I sit down or stand up. You know my every thought when far away. You chart the path ahead of me and tell me where to stop and rest. Every moment you know where I am" (Psalm 139:2-3).

If we would only get into our hearts that God is with us. God gives peace. If only I had known this as a child or how important it was to teach this to my children, instead of generations of curses, incest, and sickness. And to know that our heavenly Father knows everything about us is all the more reason to call on him in times of trouble.

Lay Down Your Burdens

"Then Jesus said, 'Come to me, all of you who are weary and carry heavy burdens, and I will give you rest'" (Matthew 11:28).

As we walk and grow in the Lord, we don't just get on top of the mountain as fast as we think. Our walk with God has been wonderful, but sometimes we have had so much baggage and still seem to, that we keep learning and getting free of things that have held us down by reading and praying about those very things that still bother us.

Many people tell things they have been through and "burdens" is the one word that always comes up. Burdens such as mothers or fathers who have guilt from spousal separations or divorce; mothers that have had abortions; fathers that have lost jobs; children that are drinking or doing drugs; someone very sick or who has lost a loved one; hearts that carry so much pain.

Jesus says, "Come to Me when you are weak and weary." You can't continue getting help with drinking or doing drugs/pills. That alone will cause more problems. This is where you call on the name of Jesus. "He gives power to those who are tired and worn out; he offers strength to the weak" (Isaiah 40:29).

Why Did Jesus Come?

Jesus came so we could know God. "For God so loved the world that he gave his only Son, so that everyone who believes in him will not perish but have eternal life" (John 3:16).

"For God sent not his Son into the world to condemn the world: but that the world through him might be saved" (John 3:17 KJV). Who are we to condemn others? We do not condemn when we have fallen in love with the people of this world. Love people! "And then he told them, Go into all the world and preach the Good News to everyone, everywhere" (Mark 16:15).

Do we love the world or the things of the world? Not when the love of the Father is in us. Since God gave, love is always in partnership. And God's greatest gift? Everlasting life or life lasting forever.

Is God at Home in My Heart?

Does God's Spirit feel comfortable in my *heart?* As the Amplified Bible says, "May Christ through your faith [actually] dwell (settle down, abide, and make His permanent home) in your hearts!" (Ephesians 3:17). "And I pray that Christ will be more and more at home in your hearts as you trust in him. May your roots go down deep into the soil of God's marvelous love" (Ephesians 3:17).

Our thoughts, our words, our actions have to be a place that God's Spirit wants to be. Sometimes we may feel like God is so far away. It is because of talking negatively about someone or holding onto something that they did to us, but God says we cannot hold on to the past. When we let go of what is past, God moves in to create our present.

Preach the Gospel

Preaching the Gospel is a divine work because it changes lives. People need the good news of the Gospel. People often need to be set free. Preach the Gospel. When the Gospel is preached correctly, people hear it and changes come. God said we are made in His image. People need to hear that the Word of God and the Holy Spirit will move them out of darkness into his marvelous light and deliverance will come.

"So as much as in me is, I am ready to preach the gospel to you for I am not ashamed of the gospel of Christ: for it is the power of God unto salvation to every one that believeth; to the Jew first, and also to the Greek" (Romans 1:15,16 KJV).

"Preach the word of God. Be persistent, whether the time is favorable or not, patiently correct, rebuke, and encourage your people with good teaching" (2 Timothy 4:2).

"I have not been afraid to speak out, as you, O Lord, well know. I have not kept this good news in my heart; I have talked about your faithfulness and saving power . . . I have told everyone in the great assembly of your unfailing love and faithfulness" (Psalm 40:9,10).

Why Would We Not Serve Jesus as Our Lord?

He awakens us every morning with blessings and we get into his Word just to find out what he has for us that day. The Bible is so full of blessings for us, for families, for friends. "Praise the Lord; praise God out savior! For each day he carries us in his arms" (Psalm 68:19). Also, "Blessed be the Lord, who daily loadeth us with benefits, even the God of our salvation" (Psalm 68:19 KJV).

It is great to lie down and just go over the Word of God that has been put into our hearts. Who can think of any reason why not to read God's letter to us and to just find all the wonderful plans he has for us now knowing our future is with our Father God. We can read something new everyday!

"Jesus responded, 'Didn't I tell you that you will see God's glory if you believe?'" (John 11:40). We have to be able to hear God's voice when the storms come against us. When sickness comes, we have to be able to speak against the sickness. How can we speak to the mountain of storms if we do not have the Word of God to fight against it? We cannot!

We have to speak God's Word through every area of our lives, through everything that we deal with daily. There is a way out with the Word! For example, sickness: sickness will not end in death. "When Jesus heard that, he said, This sickness is not unto death, but for the glory of God, that the Son of God might be glorified thereby" (John 11:4).

When we know God as our Father or as Daddy, that is real intimacy. We live in a fatherless generation. Children are growing up without a father. We feel no security if we are children without a father, but God comes to show us what the Father is like.

"Jesus told him, 'I am the way, the truth, and the life, No one can come to the Father except through me.'" (John 14:6). We need to awaken to Father God. We need to know God as Father! Father has all the power. People cannot go on without knowing how much God loves them.

No Matter What is Going on in Your Life

Refuse to give up hope. We have trials and pains in our lives. When you are hurting, say you are healed. When your home is in a mess, say it is peaceful. "Listen to me! You can pray for anything, and if You believe, you will have it" (Mark 11:24).

"How we praise God, the Father of our Lord Jesus Christ, who has blessed us with every spiritual blessing in the heavenly because we belong to Christ" (Ephesians 1:3).

Some days we may not feel like there is a reason to be joyful. Maybe that was experienced recently. We may not know why something is happening, but we can do something about it. We can start praising God, not asking for joy but praising God, and before we know it, we can be joyful. Things will took brighter and just feel better!

Find Your Personal Scripture

"Believe on the Lord Jesus and you will be saved, along with your entire household" (Acts 16:31). When you read a scripture like this pertaining to a need you may have, write it down and believe it is yours.

"Store my commands in your heart, for they will give you a long and satisfying life" (Proverbs 3:1,2). God's Word is our life. There is not one thing that we will ever go through that God hasn't got a word for. We put his Word in us to fully understand what the answer is.

Not only that, God has given each and every one of us abilities! "A spiritual gift is given to each of us as a means of helping the entire church" (1 Corinthians 12:7). A spiritual gift is given to each of us. Only believe!

Simplify Your Life!

Take time to enjoy! Keep your mind on one thing at a time. More and more does not make you happy, nor does trying to impress others. Clean clutter out of your house. Get rid of things if they are not being used. Keep what you love. Be grateful for what you have. If you do not decide to be happy, you will never be happy.

"Don't worry about anything, instead, pray about everything. Tell God what you need, and thank Him for all He has done. If you do this, you will experience God's peace, which is far more wonderful than the human mind can understand. His peace will guard your hearts and minds as you live in Christ Jesus" (Philippians 4:6,7).

Pray . . . Pray . . . Pray

There is no greater way to know our Daddy God than to pray. Read the Word of God, think of a scripture for the day, and learn to pray around it! God loves our prayers.

When there is a room full of people, for instance at church, where maybe hundreds of people are, it is just a blessing to know that God hears each and every one. But to know without a doubt he has listened to you as if you are the only one talking to him, how special that is! The God of all creation listens to you! To know you can come to God just the way you are right now is so special, too.

God is helping you to grow and to become everything he wants you to be in wellness and strength. No matter what condition you are in, he hears you! Know that you can have great peace in the midst of things going on around you. You can talk to him anytime.

"Pray at all times and on every occasion in the power of the Holy Spirit. Stay alert and be persistent in your prayers for all Christians everywhere" (Ephesians 6:18).

The Way of Love

"Love" is probably the most used word in the Bible. Our first thought is Jesus is Love, because it is so hard to have a problem with another person when you know what the Word says about love. About the time you are absolutely walking in the greatest walk of your life, you just love everyone.

The number one reason to love is because the Bible says to. We can be tested so many times in this area of our life. Jesus said, "A new commandment I give unto you. That ye love one another, as I have loved you, that ye also love one another" (John 13:34 KJV). To me, that says it all! Also, "There are three things that will endure—faith, hope, and love—and the greatest of these is love" (1 Corinthians 13:13).

When you are angry with someone remember, "Love is patient and kind, Love is not jealous or boastful or proud or rude. Love does not demand its own way. Love is not irritable, and it keeps no record of when it has been wronged. It is never glad about injustice but rejoices whenever the truth wins out. Love never gives up, never loses faith, is always hopeful, and endures through every circumstance" (1 Corinthians 13:4-8). It seems like this scripture would be our answer when we get upset!

Sometimes it can take a long time to get over being mad at someone. That is when it is so important to know the Word of God and to have the Holy Spirit to speak to our hearts. The mind will try to convince us that we have every reason to be upset.

One thing we can know for certain when we let anger come in, is we lose our joy and our peace. We can think about being wronged and think about it morning, noon, and night. But when we let the Word of God come up in our hearts and begin to speak out about love and forgiveness, then we would not be full of anger and would walk in love not even seeing the problem!

When we pray, that is when the Holy Spirit will rise up with the Word and we repent and see that person in a whole new light! It is amazing how anger clouds our minds and we feel so dark with thoughts. Then when the light of the Word gets into our minds, we see totally differently.

We can learn to cast down wrong thoughts or pictures that may come into in our mind. We can learn to plead the blood of Jesus over those wrong thoughts. When fear gets in our thoughts, plead the blood of Jesus and see the blood on the person that needs forgiving.

When we have gotten news about something pertaining to us, it can be easy to be in our own thoughts and not be sensitive to others. For instance, a bad report can cloud our minds and thoughts and cause us to do dumb things. My point is that we must try hard not to jump to get angry when we see others do what we ourselves have done. We have no idea what report someone may have gotten. Maybe they experienced a death in their family or of a friend. Maybe they are sick themselves. We have got to have patience with others.

Let us try to remember how we ourselves have needed love and forgiveness.

Heaven Is Real

Heaven is our next step. Love not the world. "Stop loving this evil world and all that it offers you, for when you love the world, you show that you do not have the love of the Father in you. And this world is fading away, along with everything it craves. But if you do the will of God, you will live forever" (1 John 2-15,17).

God is getting us ready for heaven as we are getting our own hearts right and asking the Father to forgive us of things that we have done. Desire above all to want your heart pure before you meet your heavenly Daddy. "Now may the God of peace make you holy in every way, and may your whole spirit and soul and body be kept blameless until that day our Lord Jesus Christ comes again. God, who calls you, is faithful; he will do this" (1 Thessalonians 5:23,24).

I Believe in Miracles

"Bless the Lord, O my soul: and all that is within me, bless his holy name. Bless the Lord, O my soul, and forget not all his benefits: who forgiveth all thine iniquities; who healeth all thy diseases" (Psalm 103:1-3 KJV).

We must tell ourselves *never* to forget the good things he does for us. I have been thinking about my salvation. How did I get here today 30+ years later? I can write and say God has done everything he said he would do! I pray that you learn how to believe God's Word in every area of your life, God is our hope. He is the Lover of our souls.

As the psalmist says, he forgives all our sins and heals all our diseases. I cannot count how many times since my birth into God's family that I have needed this verse. But I always had the Holy Spirit. He would tug at my heart to repent and move on. I would sometimes try so hard to do it my way but knowing what God would say, I would stay in a miser-able state until I called on Jesus for help.

"Our God is a God who saves! The Sovereign Lord rescues us from death" (Psalm 68:20). Praise God who did not ignore my prayers and did not withdraw his unfailing love from me.

A Renewed Mind

"Don't copy the behavior and customs of this world, but let God transform you into a new person by changing the way you think. Then you will know what God wants you to do, and you will know how good and pleasing and perfect his will really is" (Romans 12:2).

This means we are changed. We renew our minds with the Word of God. We read it and do it. Get understanding of the Word. Want the will of God in your life. Our think-ing must line up with God's Word. It will give us new thoughts. Feelings cannot be the boss of us any longer. "Anyone who doesn't love me will not do what I say. And remember, my words are not my own. This message is from the Father who sent me" (John 14:24).

Got to Stand on the Word of God!

God heals. Say you are healed! Do not believe a bad report.

I went through a time where I had been coughing for months and months. I finally sought medical help and was examined by three doctors. My condition was such that lying down or sitting up, I coughed; talking on the phone became difficult because I coughed; even eating was a struggle because I coughed. I was embarrassed because I coughed all the time! All through this though, I refused to walk in fear. This was the time the Word of God had to be alive in my spirit.

"Don't worry about anything; instead pray about everything. Tell God what you need, and thank him for all he has done. If you do this, you will experience God's peace, which is far more wonderful than the human mind can understand. His peace will guard your hearts and minds as you live in Christ Jesus" (Philippians 4:6-7).

There it is clearly stated that we will experience God's peace when we choose not to worry. We can know without a doubt all is well. When going through a trial, we can hear the Holy Spirit say be still. "Be silent, and know that I am God! I will be honored by every nation, I will be honored throughout the world" (Psalm 46:10).

I was then told a biopsy must be done on a suspicious spot the doctors saw on my lung thinking it was cancer. But down in my heart, I knew it was not anything. While waiting for the doctor to call to set a biopsy appointment, I heard the Holy Spirit speak clearly to my heart, "Be still!" The doctor did call later only to say the suspicious spot had shrunk. No biopsy needed!

God tells you he is with you even when three different doctors may give a bad diagnosis. That means no matter what the circumstances are like, everything will work out alright because God will never fail you or forsake you. Praise the Lord.

God speaks to our spirit. He lead us by his Spirit in us. Go to him for directions. When God speaks to our hearts, we just know to stop and listen and do. The quieter you become the more you hear from him.

Fear not, "No one will be able to stand their ground against you as long as you live. For I will be with you as I was with Moses. I will not fail you or abandon you" (Joshua 1:5). It is a miracle how God by his Spirit gives us such peace when we cry out to him during the storms in life. Let us be quick not to sit and think on the thing we are going through. Let us get our Bibles and find the answer, then speak the Word until peace takes the place where fear was.

I know that I know God has a good plan for you and me. We cannot run to someone to pray for us every time we have a trial. We have to learn to call on Jesus' name. He knows what is going to happen every minute of the day. Reread Philippians 4:6-7 about not worrying and telling God everything. God's peace is so wonderful that these verses say we let God's peace takeover our minds. What our minds think on have to be in line with what God says. Pray for the mind of Christ.

The Fear of the Lord is a Good Thing

"For I am giving you good guidance. Don't turn away from my teaching" (Proverbs 4:2).

"The fear of the Lord prolongeth days: but the years of the wicked shall be shortened" (Proverbs 10:27 KJV).

"The fear of the Lord is the beginning of wisdom: and the knowledge of the holy is understanding. For by me thy days shall be multiplied and the years of thy life shall be increased" (Proverbs 9:10-11 KJV).

The fear of the Lord means to hate all appearance of evil.

All the Gold Belongs to God

God owns all the silver and gold in the world. Not only that, we just have to believe God owns everything and believe what we read when we are having any questions. God's blessings are mine and yours! Let the Holy Spirit control our lives.

"'Bring all the tithes into the storehouse so there will be enough food in my Temple. If you do,' says the Lord Almighty, 'I will open the windows of heaven for you. I will pour out a blessing so great you won't have enough room to take it in! Try it! Let me prove it to you!'" (Malachi 3: 10).

Why tithe? "You are under a curse, for your whole nation has been cheating me." (Malachi 3:9). Our checkbook is a mirror of to whom we really belong. Our firstfruits belong to God before other things get paid. The tithe is ten percent of our income. God is in financial management! He gives us above and beyond what we can believe. Prosperity? So much so that God says, "Prove me in this . . . And I will rebuke the devourer for your sakes" (Malachi 3:10,11 KJV).

All we have has all been given by God. "Don't store up treasures here on earth, where they can be eaten by moths and get rusty, and where thieves break in and steal. Store your treasures in heaven, where they will never become moth-eaten or rusty and where they will be safe from thieves. Wherever your treasure is, there your heart and thoughts will also be" (Matthew 6:19-21). What we lay up for ourselves will one day all be gone. God is storing up what we give and we will receive 100 percent back. Trust God!

Why No Altars, God?

One of the greatest times of my Christian life was when I was newly saved and attending a small church. Altars were open after every service. I saw God move in so many ways! I brought many requests to the altars and would just cry there. I have seen many of those tearful prayers answered today. I just love the altars. I can lay all my burdens there and pray and know God hears me. What has happened to the altars? "May your will be done here on earth, just as it is in heaven" (Matthew 6:10b).

Hungry for More of Jesus

Believe for yourself that God is showering and giving so much more of his Spirit. That is what it means to be hungry for more of everything that God has for us. That hunger makes us want to spend more time with Jesus and to pray, which is to talk and to listen to him.

"God blesses you who are hungry now, for you will be satisfied" (Luke 6:21a). Once you have sat at the table with Jesus, you will never be satisfied with a little to eat. Once you have sat at the big buffet table with all the fruit you can eat, then not eating will leave you yearning for that yummy taste again. Desire to be satisfied with your soul being so full of Jesus and every good thing that comes from him.

Jesus says come and dine. "'Now come and have some breakfast!' Jesus said. And no one dared ask him if he really was the Lord because they were sure of it" (John 21:12). The Master has enough for all the needs of his servants.

We have to be hungry where we want more of Jesus, finding time to get away from being too busy with talking on the phone, shopping, or sometimes even from eating, just to spend quality time reading the Word and talking him. He will and does speak to us. Even Jesus departed into a quiet place away from everyone and things, "The next morning Jesus awoke long before daybreak and went out alone into the wilderness to pray" (Mark 1:35).

If Jesus had to stop and pray, how much more have we to stop and pray?

Following Jesus

Jesus said to pick up your cross and follow him. The victory is yours through Jesus. Resist the devil and he will flee from you. The truth is the Word of God. You are a servant of Jesus Christ. You are the sheep and he is the Shepherd. The Lord is your shepherd; you shall not want. God is with you. You shall dwell with the Lord forever and ever! God will never leave you nor forsake you.

Reading the Word of God

Reading the Bible for several years, we come across scriptures we have read many times over. Sometimes those scriptures jump into our hearts. For instance, "Above all else, guard your heart, for it affects everything you do" (Proverbs 4:23). That means from our hearts are the springs of life or the forces of life. What is important for us from going to bed to waking up is the first thing we hear in our spirit is that we have to guard our hearts everyday, sometimes several times a day.

"Pay attention, my child, to what I say. Listen carefully. Don't lose sight of my words. Let them penetrate deep within your heart, for they bring life and radiant health to anyone who discovers their meaning" (Proverbs 4:20-22). Such a powerful word to us to get in our hearts and live by.

"My child, listen to me and do as I say, and you will have a long, good life. I will teach you wisdom's ways and lead you in straight paths" (Proverbs 4:10,11). Desire more than anything else to listen and do what God is telling you. God tells us if we do what he says and if we discover and let all his words penetrate deep within our hearts, we will have a life full of blessings and radiant health.

We sometimes have to spend time and just read these verses over and over to get hold of what the Holy Spirit is saying to us. We can read a scripture over several times until we know that we know what God is saying to us. That is when we can fill up those springs of living water in our soul with life. We can do this every single day by standing on the Word.

Sometimes our hearts can get wounded so badly by what someone says or does to us, like when something comes at us and we want to think and think about it, then talk about what someone has done or said. That is the time we can stand in the midst of it and speak these words about guarding our heart. It just works. This causes us to be able to move forward and not be damaged by it. God wants us to grow and speak his Word for our lives.

We can also struggle with wanting to please people. We can learn to not have to please anyone but Jesus Christ. Desire to speak the truth and not be afraid of what someone would think or try to be a people pleaser.

Desire to speak the truth into yourself and know that God's Word is life to you. A godly boldness will develop in you from reading the Word of God over and over. Set your mind on the Word of God, not what the world says about you.

You Will Rise Again

God says you will rise again. Just know this! We know God is in us. Great heroes will come forth. "Those who are wise will shine as bright as the sky, and those who turn many to righteousness will shine like stars forever" (Daniel 12:3). We will rise to be mighty, free people. We can help free others and bring them hope. We can help others put their hands back into God's hand.

"Lord, my heart is not proud; my eyes are not haughty. I don't concern myself with matters too great or awesome for me. But I have stilled and quieted myself, just as a small child is quiet with its mother. Yes, like a small child is my soul within me" (Psalm 131:1-2). I lay my head on God's chest. I put on the full armor of Christ: the belt of truth, the shoes of peace, and the shield of faith to stop every fiery dart from the devil. (See Ephesians 6:14-17).

Take the Limits off God

Take your limits off God and let God be God! Believe you will see God do great miracles in your family, finances, and bodies. If you believe, you will receive. "No eye has seen, no ear has heard, and no mind has imagined what God has prepared for those who love him" (1 Corinthians 2:9).

We have to speak the Word of God regardless of what is going on right now. We cannot take our eyes off the Word. Our ears have to hear what God says. We cannot be hearers only but must also be doers of the Word. Desire to be a doer of the Word. "And remember, it is a message to obey, not just to listen to. If you don't obey, you are only fooling yourself" (James 1:22).

Wisdom is Life to Us as Believers!

Wisdom is full of life and offers this to us (from the book of Proverbs):

- Makes us wise. (1:23)
- Peace and safety, being unafraid. (1:33)
- Understanding. (2:3)
- Knowledge of God. (2:5)
- A shield of protection.

- Right, just, and fair.

- Joy.

- Keeps us from evil people.

- Long and satisfactory life,

- Loyalty and kindness.

- Favor with God and people.

- Good reputation.

- Renewed health and vitality. (3:8)

- Fills our barns.

- Corrects us (because he loves us).

- Happy. (3:13)

- Guidance.

- Tree of Life.

- Honor and respect.

- Keep my feet from stumbling.

- Lie down without fear.

- Not afraid of disaster.

The book of Proverbs teaches us how to live and how to have an abundance from each word of wisdom written there. Oh God, that we your children will hunger for the real things of this time here in life. "Getting wisdom is the most important thing you can do! And whatever else you do, get good judgment" (Proverbs 4:7). The Proverbs are so easy to read, but we've got to read over and over to get what the Holy Spirit wants us to know about wisdom.

Spiritual Fruit

Many mothers, fathers, and children have pain: children with divorced parents; parents on drugs; deaths in the family while young. There are probably several people whom we know that we would not think could have horrific childhood pain.

My point here is that we as Christians have to have the compassion and love of Jesus in our hearts before we can help others and pray for them. We have to have the fruit of the Spirit working in us at all times.

"But when the Holy Spirit controls our lives, he will produce this kind of fruit in us: love, joy, peace, patience, kindness, goodness, faithfulness, gentleness, and self-control. Here there is no conflict with the law" (Galatians 5:22,23). When we pray and ask God to let this fruit operate daily, we will have more compassion for others.

Patience is another spiritual fruit we have to have. Getting mad or irritated at someone because traffic is too slow or people are talking too much at the checkout line at the store when we are in a hurry. You know what I am talking about.

Plus, loving others is one spiritual fruit that is always coming up in our daily walk. The Bible says a lot about love and its importance, especially that God loves us all so much. He does know our pain, our heartaches. Jesus wants us to know how to give our burdens to him. "I know the Lord is always with me. I will not be shaken, for he is right beside me" (Psalm 16:8). When we really have the understanding of the love God has for us, we will receive his love and have the freedom of knowing who we are in him.

"Those who belong to Christ Jesus have nailed the passions and desires of their sinful nature to his cross and crucified them there. If we are living now by the Holy Spirit, let us follow the Holy Spirit's leading in every part of our lives. Let us not become conceited, or irritate one another or be jealous of one another" (Galatians 5:24-26).

The Children of God Listen

Jesus says to trust him in the depths of our being. When we settle down from being so busy with life and take the time to hear from God, our lives change in every area. "Be still and know that I am God" (Psalm 46:10a). Slow down your pace of living for awhile. Get into God's presence and you will learn to hear his voice. He says to us, "Let Me show you the way for this day." We are to relax and enjoy our lives and the presence of Jesus. He has so much to tell us. We have got to stop and listen.

God says when we pray, he will put his thoughts into our minds. We have the mind of Christ! "My child, listen to me and do as I say and you will have a long, good life" (Proverbs 4:10).

When we seek God, we can put aside thoughts and everything else. We can open our hearts and minds and receive from him. Trust God. Life will be blessed when we hear God and believe what we read in the scriptures. "Commit everything you do to the Lord, Trust him, and he will help you. Be still in the presence of the Lord, and wait patiently for him to act. Don't worry about evil people who prosper or fret about their wicked schemes" (Psalm 37:5,7).

We do not have to doubt that God will answer us. Talk to him about everything. "But I will call on God, and the Lord will rescue me. Morning, noon, and night I plead aloud in my distress, and the Lord hears my voice. He rescues me and keeps me safe from the battle waged against me, even though many still oppose me" (Psalm 55:16-18).

It Is Better to Give Than to Receive

Giving is one of the greatest blessings. Giving time praying for others when they have a need. Taking a meal or a cake to someone can also be a blessing. A door can be opened to pray for the needs of others or to ask if they know Jesus Christ as their Savior. It is refreshing to be a blessing to someone.

"Don't forget to show hospitality to strangers, for some who have done this have entertained angels without realizing it" (Hebrews 13:2).

"Don't forget to do good and to share what you have with those in need, for such sacrifices are very pleasing to God" (Hebrews 13:16).

"It is possible to give freely and become more wealthy but those who are stingy will lose everything" (Proverbs 11:24).

"The generous prosper and are satisfied; those who refresh others will themselves be refreshed" (Proverbs 12:25).

My mother-in-law told me a story I will never forget. She was cleaning the kitchen one morning when someone knocked on the door. She went to the door and saw a man who looked like a bum asking for something to eat. While she was preparing breakfast, he waited at the kitchen table. After the man ate, all at once it got quiet. She turned to see the man was no longer there! She never heard the door open or close. She looked outside but the man was nowhere to be found. She always believed an angel had visited her, which I believe, too! "Don't forget to show hospitality to strangers, for some who have done this have entertained angels without realizing it!" (Hebrews 13:2).

God's Unfailing Love in Us

From the book of Philippians:

"May God our father and the Lord Jesus Christ give you grace and peace" (1:2).

"I pray that your love for each other will overflow more and more, and that you will keep on growing in your knowledge and understanding" (1:9).

"For God is working in you, giving you the desire to obey him and the power to do what pleases him" (2:13).

"In everything you do stay away from complaining and arguing, so that no one can speak a word of blame against you" (2:14-15).

God never gives up on us. Just like with our own children, we never stop loving them. It can be so sad about what they are doing, but Jesus says he loves us and our children unconditionally.

God will give us another chance. Don't settle for less than God's best. Our God is so good and full of mercy, he says to our hearts not to be discouraged. He restores the years that have been stolen. Refresh us, Lord Jesus.

Promised Rest for God's People

From the book of Hebrews:

"For only we who believe can enter his place of rest" (4:3a).

"So God's rest is there for people to enter" (4:6a).

"Today you must listen to his voice. Don't harden your hearts against him" (4:7b).

"So there is a special rest still waiting for the people of God" (4:9).

"Let us do our best to enter that place of rest" (4:11a).

"That is why we have a great High Priest who has gone to heaven, Jesus the son of God. Let us cling to him and never stop trusting him" (4:14).

"This High Priest of ours understands our weaknesses" (4:15a).

"So let us come boldly to the throne of our gracious God. There we will receive his mercy and we will find grace to help us when we need it" (4:16).

Don't Be Offended . . . Be Like Little Children

Be good to those who hurt you. People do not always know what they are doing. Just like Job who lost everything, God restored his losses all back to him and more. (See Job 42). Trust God. "But I say love your enemies! Pray for those who persecute you!" (Matthew 5:44).

When a friend comes to see you and they are in pain or having some difficulty, don't lecture them. Listen to them. God will promote you if you forgive others. Become like a little child. Go on and do not hold bitterness or anger. Release it all to God. He will make it right!

Little children, just believe! Dream a little. Create some joy in your life. Move into the supernatural realm. God is closer than you think! Stop being so "mature" and boring. Children, just believe. Don't doubt, just believe. It is a choice. Get out of the realm of your mind and follow God's Word. So many Christians are just mad. Let it go. Turn away from this.

"The commandments of the Lord are right, bringing joy to the heart. The commands of the Lord are clear, giving insight to life" (Psalm 19:8).

Trust in God's plan for your life and future. God has great plans for you. Believe that what happens to you is for the best. God has only the best for you.

Have you ever prayed and prayed about something you wanted? It just didn't happen, but later you saw God had something so much better in his plan for you. Do you take time and thank God when you see a door close and a greater plan has worked out for you? God is in complete control of your life. He is God.

Wise Counsel

Cancel the wrong report. The words we speak are so powerful. Life and death are in the power of the tongue. Emotion cannot override what God says. When we dare to step out, our heavenly Father will not let us down! Believe and receive.

"A gossip goes around revealing secrets, but those who are trustworthy can keep a confidence" (Proverbs 11:13). Do not ever repeat what someone tells you in confidence.

Enjoy the journey. You cannot help everyone, Jesus died for you to enjoy life! Do not break the health rules by getting too busy. Do not put too much on your plate like going and going and not taking time for God or yourself. This will be a problem and you will not be happy. Blaming everyone else is not the answer. If you are not happy, do something about it. Making wise choices makes us happy.

Stop, listen, and *pray* for wisdom. Wisdom chooses to do what is right now for what will benefit us later on. Our thoughts can change. We have control to move forward.

Want more of Jesus, the Word, and the anointing? Wisdom is a must! "Cry out for insight and understanding. Search for them as you would for lost money or hidden treasure" (Proverbs 2:3).

"For the Lord grants wisdom! From his mouth come knowledge and understanding" (Proverbs 2:6).

"For wisdom will enter your heart, and knowledge will fill you with joy" (Proverbs 2:10).

The Lord Speaks to Our Hearts as He did to Moses

"But Moses pleaded with the Lord, 'O Lord, I'm just not a good speaker. I never have been, and I'm not now, even after you have spoken to me. I am clumsy with words.' 'Who makes mouths?' the Lord asked him. 'Who makes people so they can speak or not speak, hear or not hear, see or not see? Is it not I, the Lord? Now go, and do as I have told you. I will help you speak well, and I will tell you what to say'" (Exodus 5:10-12).

"Open your mouth wide, and I will fill it with good things" (Psalm 81:10b).

God speaks to our hearts and prepares us to speak for him. Stand on these verses before you speak to people or speak at a meeting. God knows what each listener has need to hear. Trust in him to speak through you and let his Spirit speak to people's hearts. Salvations, healings, deliverance come from God. Let him fill your heart with his Word to speak for him.

Wrong Confessions

When we see Jesus our desires change. The devil does not know anything about us. We tell him with our words. Our words should line up with God's promises. If we speak death, sickness, or lack it is the devil's language and he sends his demons. Stop and say what God says. He gives his angels charge over our words.

The devil hates for us to be blessed. We have to do spiritual warfare. If God is for us, who can be against us? Blessing and cursing should not come out of the same mouth. This is wrong! Life and death are in the power of the tongue. Our tongue can loose torment on others. We should bless them instead.

This is a good reason to pray in the spirit! We are talking to God in another language. He knows our thoughts and if we are angry or upset with someone, praying in the spirit releases God's anointing and love for someone we cannot love in ourselves. But God will cause a spirit of love to cover the sin that so easily besets us. Let God fill our thoughts and hearts with his love for others.

Speak Life

Be careful how you talk about yourself. You will never rise above your own confession. What you say goes to the spiritual realm. Line up your mouth with the Word of God. Your fruit will be so good! Who are you to disrespect what God made? Get over it! Do not compare yourself with anyone. You are not weird; you are unique. Be careful how you talk about God.

"Then those who feared the Lord spoke with each other and the Lord listened to what they said. In his presence, a scroll of remembrance was written to record the names of those who feared him and loved to think about him" (Malachi 3:16). God is faithful! He is good to us.

Talking about People

Be careful how you talk about people. Do not fault people. Do not tell anything bad you know about others. Use self-control. Cover your friends. Three brothers were told the facts about their father; two covered him up. (See Genesis 9:20-27).

"So get rid of all malicious behavior and deceit. Don't just pretend to be good! Be done with hypocrisy and jealousy and backstabbing. You must crave pure spiritual milk so that you can grow into the fullness of your salvation. Cry out for this nourishment as a baby cries for milk, now that you have had a taste of the Lord's kindness" (1 Peter 2:1-2).

"Don't grumble about each other, my brothers and sisters, or God will judge you. For look! The great Judge is coming. He is standing at the door!" (James 5:9). It is none of our business. It is between them and God.

With God All Things are Possible

"He replied, 'What is impossible from a human perspective is possible with God'" (Luke 18:27).

"For I can do everything with the help of Christ who gives me the strength I need" (Philippians 4:13).

"May the grace of the Lord Jesus Christ be with your spirit" (Philippians 4:23).

Love to read the Word and to find scriptures. Jesus Christ knows every need we have and has a word for it. Say yes to the Word of Life and Truth. "Let your roots grow down into him and draw up nourishment from him, so you will grow in faith, strong and vigorous in the truth you were taught. Let your lives overflow with thanksgiving for all he has done" (Colossians 2:7).

You are entitled to these blessings. You are about to walk in your blessings. You can ask for rain-blessings! The rain will loosen up some stuff in your life. Rain will wash you! You are entitled to God's blessings. I pray as you read this, that you just believe and receive your healing, forgiveness, and blessings that our Father has for you. You are a blessing to the ones around you.

Promises, Promises, Promises

"Give your burdens to the Lord, and he will take care of you. He will not permit the godly to slip and fall" (Psalm 55:22). God says we are his at all times. And when we get this in our heart, not one thing can stop us from receiving his protection.

Pray to give your cares and problems to Jesus. He will take them from you and give you such peace. This sounds almost too easy, but it requires a deep level of trust knowing God's way is perfect.

"I am leaving you with a gift—peace of mind and heart. And the peace I give isn't like the peace the world gives. So don't be troubled or afraid" (John 14:27).

Do Not Lose Your Confidence

The enemy likes to steal your joy. "So do not throw away this confident trust in the Lord, no matter what happens, Remember the great reward it brings you! Patient endurance is what you need now, so you will continue to do God's will. Then you will receive all that he has promised" (Hebrews 10:35-36).

Do not throw away your confidence. Keep your confidence in the middle of a trial. Continue to declare what God had promised you! Your confidence has to stay high. It will give you victory when the enemy comes in to steal the Word. God is the same regardless of what the devil does. God is still the same.

The Word of God will be performed in your fife. Lose confidence and you lose your joy, praise, and promise. Keep your confidence active at all times and keep your heart right with God. "Dear friends, if our conscience is clear, we can come to God with bold confidence. And we will receive whatever we request because we obey him and the things that please him" (1 John 3:21-22).

The Words of Our Mouths

There is a way that seems right to man, but not with God. Walk in line with God's Word! The biggest problem we have is not speaking what the Word of God says. The book of James says our mouth gets us in trouble (see James 2:1-11). Speaking the opposite of what God says, we lose everything. But speak the Word and we will have all God promises us. We need to renew our minds. We cannot ask for a promise if we do not know the promises.

I Am Rich in God's Blessings and Favor

Expect great things from God. Cheer yourself up. Live with a holy expectancy. Be expecting good from God. Wealth! God's favor! What is favor? God's kindness and help toward you, promotion, and supernatural increase. Heaven is not governed by earth. Walk in God's favor. It causes people to go out of their way to bless you. The impossible favor of God is working in your life now, bestowing to you and your families. "For the Lord God is our sun and our shield. He gives us grace and glory. The Lord will withhold no good thing from those who do what is right" (Psalm 84:11).

Don't Judge Others

"Stop judging others, and you will not be judged. For others will treat you as you treat them" (Matthew 7:1,2a).

"Do for others what you would like them to do for you. This is a summary of all that is taught in the law and the prophets" (Matthew 7:12).

"But when you are praying, first forgive anyone you are holding a grudge against, so that your Father in heaven will forgive your sins, too" (Mark 11: 2 5).

We have to be sure to forgive quickly. The quickest way to lose our joy is by holding a grudge. We can take a word someone has said and totally turn it around from what it started out to be. Forgiving others has to be important to us because we want God to forgive us when we sin.

We grieve the Holy Spirit by holding on to something and not giving our problems, anger, or judgment to him. He is our Counselor. Go to God before we start talking to everyone about what someone has done to us.

"A fool is quick-tempered, but a wise person stays calm when insulted" (Proverbs 12:16). We all have been insulted by someone, but we have to learn not to let those words get into our hearts. It is hard not to tell what someone has said about us. A story gets twisted when it starts traveling around.

When I was first born again, I wrote all the scriptures I could find about gossiping, unforgiveness, grudges, and the like. I found out God is not pleased with our words when we repeat over and over what someone said about others or ourselves.

Forgiveness is not easy, but if we want to hear from God, we have to forgive, to let it go fast. Words fester and cause sickness to our souls. We must take personal responsibility for what we do with what we hear.

I have learned from a dear friend that when gossiping starts to ask, "Were you there to witness this?" Generally the answer is no, but in any case just learn not to listen to the gossip. Get up and leave the conversation.

Let's desire to be like the wise woman in the book of Proverbs. "She opens her mouth with wisdom and in her tongue is the law of kindness" (Proverbs 31:26 KJV).

Do Not Be Afraid

Do not let unexpected events throw you off course. Instead, respond calmly and confidently, remembering that God is with you. As soon as something grabs your attention, talk to God about it. Thus he shares your joys and your problems; he helps you through whatever is before you. This is how he lives in you and works through you. This is the way of peace.

"They do not fear bad news; they confidently trust the Lord to care for them" (Psalm 112:7). "Don't be afraid for I am with you, Do not be dismayed for I am Your God, I will strengthen you. I will help you. I will uphold you with my victorious right hand" (Isaiah 41:10).

Have a Humble and Gentle Spirit

We have been called by God. God hears the humble in heart. "Be humble and gentle. Be patient with each other, making allowance for each other's faults because of your love. Always keep yourselves united in the Holy Spirit, and bind yourselves together with peace" (Ephesians 4:2-3).

"In the same way, you wives must accept the authority of your husbands, even those who refuse to accept the Good News. Your godly lives will speak to them better than any words. They will be won over by watching your pure, godly behavior. You should be known for the beauty that comes from within, the unfading beauty of a gentle and quiet spirit, which is so precious to God" (1 Peter 3:1,2,4).

Minister to Others

Be able to give to another, then you will be strengthened. Give the advantage, not take it. If you are spiritually broke, you are needy. Needy people scare people. It is too much drama. Boldness is to be shared with someone else. Minister to others your boldness, releasing something to someone else.

We cannot do one thing without God's anointing. Not walking in love is the only thing that keeps us from the anointing. If we get away from the truth, we have to repent and ask forgiveness first. Believe in the power of prayer. Keeping our hearts and minds on Jesus gives us the anointing. We can pray for someone, give them a word, or just talk to Jesus for ourselves!

The Harder You Fall, the Higher the Bounce!

Was I born like this? "For I was born a sinner—yes, from the moment my mother conceived me" (Psalm 51:5). We all have the same right to choose to change. Our job is to help people. Life or death is everyone's choice. True freedom is choosing Jesus. Even though sin is passed down through generations, the good news is the blood of Jesus makes us free to walk away from the sin.

God has put something in us to make us strong. We have a heavenly Daddy that has given us so much strength to go through trials, pain, or sickness. We have just got to stand on his Word. We cannot believe a bad report. Believe only what God says about us. We must get his Word in our hearts! If God is for us who can be against us? We are the head not the tail, above and not below.

The Rock Is Jesus

Know that Jesus Christ is the Rock of your salvation. Think of a rock to hide under when you have to pray or intercede. Know the solid rock will never move. It is always there for you. "The Lord continued 'Stand here on this rock beside me. As my glorious presence passes by I will put you in the cleft of the rock and cover you with my hand until I have passed'" (Exodus 33:21-22).

There may be many times you have to go to the cleft of the rock to cry when you need to pray. "No one is holy like the Lord! There is no one besides you; there is no Rock like our God" (1 Samuel 2:2).

"The Lord is my rock, my fortress, and my savior; My God is my rock, in whom I find protection. He is my shield, the strength of my salvation, and my stronghold" (Psalm 18:2). A stronghold is a fortified place, a place of security or survival. You sometimes need protection against your mind when you get a report of sickness or disease. But the report can change! "No, despite all these things, overwhelming victory is ours through Christ, who loved us" (Romans 8:37). The doctor may come out after surgery and say that there is cancer. But the report can change. If God is for you, who can be against you?

Jesus Christ loves you so much. He will never change. He is your solid foundation. "Seek the Lord, and his strength, seek his face evermore" (Psalm 105:4).

Jesus says to his children, "Trust Me with your life. I have a good plan for you." Don't walk in fear or doubt— just put your trust in Jesus and watch him make your crooked paths straight! Trust Jesus.

A Prayer

"God, I believe your heart has shown me the seriousness of talking about someone. God, I pray that my heart will be pure and holy until I see you in heaven. God, you mean business with your Word; I want to retain what I read and know what is right at this hour. I do not want to hurt anyone or repeat what I hear about anyone. I believe that it is so wrong to repeat what I hear about others. The story probably has no truth to it. Please God, let me know in my heart when I sin with my mouth or thoughts. I don't want to be in a conversation and agree with anyone talking about someone. Help me to be like Jesus. Amen."

"Let me live so I can praise you, and may your laws sustain me" (Psalm 119:175). "I have hidden your word in my heart, that I might not sin against you" (Psalm 119:11).

The Blood of Jesus

Nothing would be available to us without the blood of Jesus. We know who we are because of the blood of Jesus. We are delivered from the opinions of people. We are Blood Christians and can plead the blood daily over ourselves, our family, our friends.

Know your rights by the blood! Know about the blood. Believe in the blood. Appropriate the power of the blood by faith. Receive your healed marriage by the blood of Jesus, see your children restored, receive your victory, get bills paid, children's bills paid. God is our only source. Trust him only! God is our one source. Things could get worse, but trust God. Rise out of the ashes. Rise out of trouble. Let go. Plead the blood over everything. Expect a miracle. This is your day.

"For you know that God paid a ransom to save you from the empty life you inherited from your ancestors. And the ransom he paid was not mere gold or silver. He paid for you with the precious lifeblood of Christ, the sinless, spotless Lamb of God" (1 Peter 1:18,19).

The blood is precious when you have lack. It redeems, it delivers from the devil and the power of darkness. Jesus paid the price with his own blood. We are delivered from the power of darkness by the blood.

The blood has purchased our redemption and inheritance. "Always thanking the Father, who has enabled you to share the inheritance that belongs to God's holy people, who live in the light. For he has rescued us from the one who rules in the kingdom of darkness, and he has brought us into the Kingdom of his dear Son. God has purchased our freedom with his blood and has forgiven all our sins" (Colossians 1:12-14).

The blood of Jesus ensures that Satan has *no* more power over us. Forgiveness of sin is ours by the blood. There is nothing so bad that Jesus has not washed it away. God wants to walk with us. There is no more guilt. Let no one accuse you of anything. We are no more a slave to darkness. "So if the Son sets you free, you will indeed be free" (John 8:36). Free indeed. Freedom has come to us. We are forever free by the blood of Jesus!

God Is with Us
Psalm 139

We can have our ways, our plans, and desires. We can hide our heart from people, but not from God. He sees and hears everything we do. There are no secrets from God. We cannot escape from God's love! And because of his great love for us, we can confess our wrongs and be forgiven. Stand still and see the glory of God.

Are you afraid of the dark? God is there. Are you afraid of enemies? God can take care of them. Our God is an awesome God. Do you have fear because the path before you is full of danger? You serve a God that will answer you. No good thing will he withhold from you, and he will *not* leave you nor forsake you. He is a friend that sticks closer than a brother.

Let Your Life Be Filled with God's Light

This is a new day! Seek the Kingdom of God. Coming around the corner, something is about to happen. You can now hear things differently. So seek first the Kingdom of God and his righteousness. Believe you receive exactly what God has for you. The Holy Spirit will show you things to come.

God is light! "This is the message he has given us to announce to you: God is light and there is no darkness in him at all" (John 1:5). Your faith will be energized if you walk in the light you have. God is light! Light means to do what you know is right. In God's grace and mercy, he cleanses you when you repent.

Do not judge someone else because you do not know how much of the light has been given to another. Do not criticize. "Dear friends, if our conscience is clear, we can come to God with bold confidence. And we will receive whatever we request because we obey him and do the things that please him" (1 John 3:21-22).

PART FOUR

Seven Steps to Receive Emotional Healing

Bless the Lord, oh my soul and forget not all his benefits; Who forgiveth all thine iniquities; Who healeth all the diseases; Who redeemeth thy life from destruction; Who cowneth thee with lovingkindness and tender mercies.

—Psalms 103: 2-4

Seven Steps to Receive Your Emotional Healing

1. Ask Jesus Christ into your heart.

   "For God so loved the world that he gave his only Son, so that everyone who believes in him will not perish but have eternal life" (John 3:16).

2. After receiving Jesus into your heart, you will be different! Cares will lift off you!

   "Therefore if any man be in Christ, he is a new creature: old things are passed away, behold, all things are become new" (2 Corinthians 5:17 KJV). This also reads: "What this means is that those who become Christians become new persons. They are not the same inside anymore, for the old life is gone. A new life has begun!" (2 Corinthians 5:17).

3. Become very hungry for the Word of God!

   "Thy words were found, and I did eat them; and thy word was unto me the joy and rejoicing of mine heart: for I am called by thy name, O Lord God of hosts" (Jeremiah 15:16 KJV). All scripture is inspired by God and is useful to teach us what is true, and to make us realize what is wrong in our lives. It straightens us out and teaches us to do what is right. It is God's way of preparing us in every way, fully equipped for every good thing God wants us to do" (2 Timothy 3:16,17).

4. Become willing to follow wherever God leads. God orders our steps daily. You will have doors open to you to speak life into others.

"Go to now, ye that say today or tomorrow we will go into such a city, and continue there a year, and buy and sell, and get gain: whereas ye know not what shall be on the morrow. For what is your life? It is even a vapour, that appeareth for a little time, and then vanisheth away. For that ye ought to say, If the Lord will, we shall live, and do this, or that" (James 4:13-15 KJV). "The steps of the godly are directed by the Lord. He delights in every detail of their lives" (Psalm 37:23).

5. Seek wisdom. Choose life and blessing.

"For the Lord giveth wisdom: out of his mouth cometh knowledge and understanding. He layeth up sound wisdom for the righteous: he is a buckler (shield) to them that walk uprightly" (Proverbs 2:6,7 KJV). "Choose to love the Lord your God and to obey him, and commit yourself to him, for he is your life" (Deuteronomy 30:20a).

6. Allow healing and miracles for your body. God's Word brings health and is like medicine to your flesh.

"My child, pay attention to what I say. Listen carefully to my words. Don't lose sight of them. Let them penetrate deep into your heart, for they bring life to those who find them, and healing to their whole body" (Proverbs 4:20-22).

7. Find your identity in God and thus have freedom with God.

   Freedom is one of the greatest gifts that we can receive from our Father God! He takes broken vessels and makes them into the children of God he so desires us to be. This freedom allows us to see ourselves as very special to him, resulting in not being concerned about trying to please people—that is the greatest freedom. Relying on ourselves can lead to insecurities that among other things can cause us to want everyone to like us. Learning to rely on God and knowing when to say no is such freedom. When we understand the love God has for us, we will receive his love and have the freedom of knowing who we are in him.

Forgiveness Leads to Healing

Yes, we have to believe God's Word about everything in our lives, including our relationship with him, what to do with our emotions or stress or sickness.

With regard to our emotions, our body picks up the messages our emotions send it. For instance, we think we can bury emotional pain so deep, but our body knows when we are holding on to it. We have to forgive others so we can be healed from the pains. In my case, I spoke blessings over my parents even when my mind cried out not to, and I saw healings in my own body! God's Word, God's way of doing things, sets us free from the pain. This comes from our relationship with him. "Pay attention, my child, to what I say. Listen carefully. Don't lose sight of my words, Let them penetrate deep within your heart, for they bring life and radiant health to anyone who discovers their meaning" (Proverbs 4:20-22).

When something bad happens, when fear comes, we tend to shut it up in our hearts, i.e. the bad things, the pain. But when someone offends us, Jesus says to forgive them.

Yet, we want to get even sometimes and talk negatively about them. However, remember God forgives us of all our trespasses. When we have something against anyone, forgive them so that our heavenly Father may forgive us.

God says we cannot get forgiveness for ourselves. We have to go to him. We have to give all offenses to God because unforgiveness blocks fellowship with him. That means God must withhold from us many blessings that might otherwise come to us. We don't have to feel like forgiving. Forgiveness is not an emotion but a decision.

Jesus has the perfect plan for us. Don't try to figure it out, Give your pains to Jesus; watch him do what he said he would do for you. For many years while growing up, I would bite my fingernails. I also had clutched fists-holding on to pain and shame. But my hands are open now to receive blessings from my Father God.

God will hear you when you ask him for help. Ask him to give you grace to forgive-you will and you can do it. You will have the mind of Christ to understand his Word. You will be a blessing to someone. God will use you to hear the pain of someone else and you will pray for them for their healing! Praise God. He wants you to be free and bless others.

In the book of John, we are told to confess our sins and God will forgive us. (See 1 John 1:9.) Sometimes, we need to forgive God! We think he did something to us. Simply say, "God, I forgive you." Don't blame God. At the cross,

Jesus forgave the people persecuting him. Please forgive others today. Freedom is yours today!

Living in dependence on Jesus is the greatest abundant life we could ever ask for. God wants us to trust him for everything. We can have freedom from pain, neglect, abuse, weakness, loneliness, or fear. But we have to watch how we respond to others. Some of our problems can be and are rooted in us! We have to go before God and ask him to show us if there is anything we need to deal with, Sometimes things can upset us; sometimes, it is the truth that we have not dealt with.

The enemy does all he can to keep us in the darkness, When we see an issue that keeps coming up, pray and ask God to bring the light to get free from it. We want to be free from everything that is not godly in us. God loves us and wants us to have freedom to be who he wants us to be.

This Too Shall Pass

The good news is no matter how dismal our current situation or outlook, we are assured by God, "This too shall pass." Put on the full armor of God. (See Ephesians 6:10-18.) The enemy will attack us when we are weak and will try to run over us. He never stops telling us we will never amount to anything. He will tell us we are not as good-looking as others or that we are sick or a multitude of other wrong things. Well, remember this—he is a liar! "The thief cometh not, but for to steal, and to kill, and to destroy: I am come that they might have life, and that they might have it more abundantly" (John 10:10 KJV).

It is so important to find a Christian that knows how to pray. Pray for kingdom friends that know how to plead the blood of Jesus over you. We have to know whose voice we are listening to. Is it Father God or the enemy? Jesus said a stranger's voice we will not follow. "The gatekeeper opens the gate for him, and the sheep hear his voice and come to him. He calls his own sheep by name and leads them out. After he has gathered his own flock, he walks ahead of them, and they follow him because they recognize his voice. They won't follow a stranger; they will run from him because they don't recognize his voice" (John 10:3-5).

We will know God's voice—it is so precious. When we become like Jesus, we will love like he does. "My prayer for all of them is that they will be one, just as you and I are one, Father—that just as you are in me, and I am in you, so they will be in us, and the world will believe you sent me" (John 17:21). One with the Father. We will have a love for others to see.

"Above all else, guard your heart, for it affects everything you do" (Proverbs 4:23). Learn to guard your heart. Do not accept everything that is said which does not line up with the Bible. Know who you are in Christ.

When someone says something about you and you know it is not God's Word about you, stop the words coming at you. Perhaps like me, you have heard someone tell you how dumb you were. I was often told as a child, "You'll never amount to anything." But now I am a child of God. I know that his love is more than my mind can comprehend, but I also know that he is so in love with me that those ugly words from childhood do not have any power over my thought life anymore.

Before I left Texas, I went to the courthouse to get some information. I asked the lady working there if I could read the papers about me. Because of favor with her, she let me read those papers. You see, the words "poor white trash" were something that always stuck in my mind growing up at the children's home and later into life. Sure enough, those very words were written in the files about me.

Then, to hear a doctor say of my future that I would never have children after what my father did to me. *Wrong!* I have two beautiful, healthy sons! To hear I would lose my mind, *wrong!* I've got the mind of Christ! To hear "poor white trash." *Wrong!* And to hear that I would never amount to anything, *wrong!* My Father God is the King of Kings! I belong to Him.

Reject negative words. We never want to come in agreement with something that is not from God's Word. When we hear something that does not line up with what God says, we can quickly say in our hearts we do not receive that! This is another reason why it is so important to know God's Word. God wants to be central in our minds. His peace displaces negative words, he wants his Spirit to have control over our hearts and minds at all times. May our thoughts and spoken words be flavored with God's Word!

"Those who love me inherit wealth, for I fill their treasuries" (Proverbs 8:21). Like me, you can have something that money can't buy. You can have so much peace and joy in life knowing who you are in him. The love of Jesus is in your heart! He watches over you. He never leaves you nor forsakes you. "Your enemies will stay far away; you will live in peace. Terror will not come near" (Isaiah 54:14).

God says that your enemies will always be defeated because he is on your side. What you can say is, "Thank you, God, for my wonderful life that is covered with the blood and blessings of Christ!"

Inspirational Thoughts

- God is a God of the heart. He sees our heart.

- Reason is never required. Faith opens the door.

- What's in your heart is what comes out.

- Obey the Bible and peace will come.

- God gave us his word to make us overcomers in everything.

- When you praise God, he will show up.

- We are complete now. We are righteous now!

- God's Word is so full of blessings that always there is a word when we need to hear from him.

- Giving is one of life's greatest blessings. It is refreshing to be a blessing to someone.

- It is dangerous to follow feelings. Pressure leads into compromise.

- All sin begins with a lie.

- We stay strong when we stay little in our hearts.

- If Jesus had to stop and pray, how much more have we to stop and pray?

- Love needs to be released. Everything works by love.

- Along with strengths, we also have weaknesses. Let Jesus Christ be strong in your weaknesses; let Him be your strength on your weak days.

- Break the power of negative words. Instead bless people.

- We cannot live by feelings nor believe them. Live by the Word of God!

- God guides us along the right paths bringing honor to his name.

- Live out of your spirit.

- Give yourself to one thing: seeking the Kingdom of God.

- Let God's glory be *big* in your life.

- Turn all your problems over to God. Cast over all your cares to Jesus.

- God loves to hear the sound of our voices.

- Open your heart and let God fix it.

- Let us try to remember how we ourselves have needed love and forgiveness.

- Jesus Christ is God's love gift to the world. And believers are the Father's love gift to Jesus Christ.

- God never makes a mistake.

❖ The quieter you become, the more you hear from God.

❖ God speaks to our spirit.

❖ Read the Word of God, think of a scripture for the day, and learn to pray around it!

❖ God gave gifts; one is not better than the other.

❖ Praising God means you are thanking him for what he will do!

❖ Get the Word of God in you to have a life of blessings.

❖ The most damaging thing a Christian can do is talk negatively about others.

❖ God's love is the beginning of how to give love and receive. God is love.

❖ Pray about everything!

❖ Whatever God asks you to do, do it.

❖ Let heaven fill your thoughts.

About the Author

Dana Cryer is an accomplished author, speaker, and dedicated Christian. Her life is a living testimony of God's amazing power to deliver. After having suffered years of mental, physical, and sexual abuse, Dana was on the verge of suicide when God miraculously delivered her, gloriously saved her, and called her to minister to those who are oppressed, abused, and emotionally wounded. She has a heart for hurting people and has dedicated her life to sharing hope, encouragement, and God's unconditional love to people everywhere. Dana has been married for more than 45 years and has two grown sons.